I0155332

Restoring

Lost

Treasures

Back to the Last-Days

Church

McDougal & Associates
Servants of Christ and Stewards of the
Mysteries of God

Restoring Lost Treasures

Back to the Last-Days Church

A Call to Awaken the Army of God

By

BILLY WEBRE

Published by:

McDougal & Associates
www,ThePublishedWord.com

McDougal & Associates is dedicated to spreading the Gospel of the Lord Jesus Christ to as many people as possible in the shortest time possible.

ISBN: 978-1-964665-00-9

Printed on demand in the U.S., the U.K. and Australia
For Worldwide Distribution

Acknowledgements

I would like to thank my wife Toni for her many years of service to the Lord as a faithful follower of Jesus Christ and to me as my loving wife. Being fellow laborers in the work of the Kingdom and walking this road together has taught me to be more tender toward others, more patient, and less confrontational, to listen more and to talk less. It was your example that taught me to care more for others, to stop and see what was going on before reacting.

I am forever grateful for you being my encourager and my caregiver in the times when I couldn't care for myself. You have given more than you have taken and mothered many as you truly cared for others and taught them by your loving actions.

As I was writing this book, you heard my heart when I was sharing what the Lord was speaking to me. You wept with me as the weight of God's revelation poured through us together. I am so thankful for you as we pursue many more years together, working for the Kingdom and loving people. I have every assurance that one day we will reap our reward in the presence of a loving Savior.

CONTENTS

THE TIME IS COMING WHEN
PEOPLE WON'T LISTEN TO GOOD
TEACHING. INSTEAD, THEY WILL
LOOK FOR TEACHERS WHO WILL
PLEASE THEM BY TELLING THEM
ONLY WHAT THEY ARE ITCHING
TO HEAR. THEY WILL TURN
FROM THE TRUTH AND EAGERLY
LISTEN TO SENSELESS STORIES.
— 2 TIMOTHY 4:3-4, CEV

INTRODUCTION

What a privilege it is to live as a believer in these uncertain times and be a part of the last-days army of God! We are living in a dark period that was predicted many places in the Word of God. As it gets darker and darker around us, it is the Church that should be getting brighter. The Gospel should become more effective, and the power of God should be more evident in the Church as we draw nearer to our blessed hope of redemption. The Church should be a beacon of hope to a lost and dying world. God's Church should be made up of those that know their God and do mighty exploits.

However, many in the Body of Christ have been put to sleep spiritually. The cross is very seldom being preached these days, and salvation has been cheapened to a simple formula of just saying a short prayer, without people truly being sorrowful enough to repent or change their ways. The call to be true disciples who would be willing to lay down their life, take up their cross, and leave their past behind is very seldom part of the mandate of becoming a lifelong believer.

In fact, many leaders in the church have made the message of the cross into a mockery of true Christianity. Numbers are now the mark of a successful church, and this brings with it the necessity of having to tickle the ears of those not willing to change their life and allowing them to submit to the culture around them. Not offending either believers or unbelievers seems to be the method of ministry used to grow and maintain the numbers of those attending church services.

As we maneuver through these difficult times, we, as true believers, see inconsistencies, compromise, and a church that is not prepared for the last-days battle that is now taking place for the souls of men.

While many attend church, the world, for the most part, is not interested in what the church now has to offer. Something must change drastically or there will be many who will not make it to their heavenly destination.

I will attempt to share in this book the revelation that God gave o me as to why we, as the Body of Christ, need transformation before that great and dreadful Day of the Lord. The things that I write here are not new, but they are fresh from the throne of God, from the very heart of God, and they are for the Church of God. Please read this word from the Lord with humility and openness and hear what the Spirit of the Lord is saying to the church today. May we desire and seek a fresh outpouring of the presence of God in our personal lives, in our ministries, and in our church gatherings.

I have written this book so that the Body of Christ will be informed and awakened to the plot of the enemy to steal the inheritance that our Lord and Savior has paid a dear price for, by shedding His precious blood.

I want to address two groups of people: church leaders and members of the Body of Christ as a whole.

CHURCH LEADERS

If you are in a role of leadership and are responsible to shepherd those whom God has placed in your care, it is your responsibility to be very diligent to preach what is needed to bring about change and maturity in the Body of Christ in this troubling time. We cannot disregard the Scriptures for the sake of not offending people God has given to us to raise up.

On the day that we all stand before the Judgement Seat of Christ, we will be held accountable for how we have led those precious souls that Jesus has entrusted to us. We know that the Church is His Bride, and therefore the well-being of the Church is serious business to Him.

THE MEMBERS OF THE BODY
OF CHRIST AS A WHOLE

We, as the Body of Christ, must open our eyes and have hears to hear what the Spirit is saying and doing today. 2 Timothy 4:3-4 says:

For the time will come when they will not endure sound doctrine, but after their own lust shall they heap to themselves teachers, having itching ears. And they shall turn their ears from the truth and shall be turned unto fables.

As the world gets darker, many are offended by the truth in God's Word. This leads some believers to find a gospel that is not offensive to their modern way of life and belief system. There must be an awakening to the reality that Jesus is coming back for a glorious Church without spot or wrinkle.

This book is an attempt to speak truth to the lies of the culture that blinds many good people to the reality that one day Jesus just might say to them, "Depart from Me, I never knew you." This is a time for the church to shine with the brightness of the glory of God, to be the beacon of hope to a lost world that is skeptical of the things of God.

> **AS THE WORLD GETS DARKER, MANY ARE OFFENDED BY THE TRUTH IN GOD'S WORD. THIS LEADS SOME BELIEVERS TO FIND A GOSPEL THAT IS NOT OFFENSIVE TO THEIR MODERN WAY OF LIFE AND BELIEF SYSTEM!**

The Church is to adorn herself with the brightness of God's presence. We are to be those who demonstrate the power, love, and compassion of a dedicated army, ready to do battle with the enemy. The Church is to be made up of fierce deliverers of those in bondage, setting the captive free and bringing healing to the masses, just like Jesus did. We are to do the *"greater works"* (see John 14:12). Our gatherings should be a powerful manifestation of the Spirit, full of life and freedom.

We are to take a stand against the sins of the culture, the lies of the enemy, and the compromises in the Body of Christ. Our meetings should be a training ground for those who desire to grow spiritually, activating the gifts in the lives of each believer, so that they can be effective in their world. We, as the Church, should be in a constant state of training, discipling, equipping, and releasing the army of God into the world around them, so that this glorious Gospel can be heard by all those who have ears to hear.

The ministry that God placed on my heart many years ago is called REACH Ministries. REACH stands for five things the Lord has given me as a mandate to do at this critical time:

Restore the Church back to God's original plan for His Church,

Evangelize the lost and raise up soul winners for a last-days awakening,

Assemble the Church as one united force to reach the lost in our communities.

Care for the needs of those who are desperate and in despair, bringing
Healing and deliverance to those who are
   broken, hurting, addicted, and sick.

This book is a call to restore the Church back to God's original design, the way Jesus and His disciples did ministry. I am both humbled and fearful to have to write these things to the Body of Christ. In no way am I an authority or the first or last written word on this subject. I am only writing as the Lord has given me the unction of the Holy Spirit to write. I do not claim to know all there is to know about restoring the Church back to God's original design, but I do feel that this subject is one of the mandates that I am responsible to give to the Body of Christ at this particular time.

I have discovered that there are treasures that have been lost, treasures that the church must pursue, seek out, and dedicate their lives to find once again, just as treasure hunters would pursue gold lost in the depths of the sea. It is God's will that the

Church should bring these hidden treasures back to where they belong.

In this book, we will discover treasures lost long ago that have a lot to do with what is going on today. We will also see God's original design for the Church, what the enemy has been doing to stop the Church from being effective in our world, and how to restore what has been missing for so many year.

It is time for the Church to be real, accepting no substitutes, bringing back the treasures that have been hidden so that we can do God's work in God's way!

Billy Webre
Gray, Louisiana

IT IS TIME FOR THE CHURCH TO BE REAL, ACCEPTING NO SUBSTITUTES, BRINGING BACK THE TREASURES THAT HAVE BEEN HIDDEN SO THAT WE CAN DO GOD'S WORK GOD'S WAY!

CHAPTER 1

THE ARK OF GOD'S PRESENCE

Take this book of the law, and put it in the side of the ark of the covenant of the LORD your God, that it may be there for a witness against thee.

Deuteronomy 31:26

The Ark of the Covenant has always fascinated me. As a young man, just married, I remember my wife and I being excited to go to the movies to watch, "Raiders of the Lost Ark." That movie was a thriller, a sit-on-the-edge-of-your-seat kind of film. It appealed to me because of the many Bible references in it. Because I was raised in church and my mother taught me the stories of the Ark and the Tabernacle in the wilderness, I was amazed at how the Lord had showed up for the children of Israel.

I remembered the story of how a cloud had settled over the Tabernacle because of the presence of the Ark in the Holy of Holies. I imagined the fire that lit up the night sky as all the tents of God's people made it the center of their encampment in the wilderness. I had always wondered what it would have been like to live in those days, experiencing the presence of God every day.

When I eventually became a pastor, I purchased a painting of the Tabernacle in the wilderness with the fire of God shining forth from the Most Holy Place and the Ark of the Covenant up into the clouds overhead. That painting was a reminder to me that God wanted to show up in every service we conducted or attended.

I studied the Ark of God's presence, wanting God to show up as He had in the wilderness and on the Day of Pentecost in the book of Acts. I realize that the Ark was only a representation of God on earth and that it was a vital part of the old covenant made with the children of Israel and was God showing up and showing off. But it was also a type and symbol of the new covenant that Jesus would make with those who believed on Him.

> **THE ARK WAS ONLY A REPRESENTATION OF GOD ON EARTH AND WAS A VITAL PART OF THE OLD COVENANT MADE WITH THE CHILDREN OF ISRAEL, BUT IT WAS ALSO A TYPE AND SYMBOL OF THE NEW COVENANT THAT JESUS WOULD MAKE WITH THOSE WHO BELIEVED ON HIM!**

Colossians 1:26-29, CEV

*For ages and ages this message was kept secret from everyone, but now it has been explained to God's people. God did this because he wanted you Gentiles to understand his wonderful and glorious mystery. And the mystery is that **Christ lives in you**, and he is your hope of sharing in God's glory.*

We announce the message about Christ, and we use all our wisdom to warn and teach everyone, so that all of Christ's followers will grow and become mature. That's why I work so hard and use the mighty power he gives me.

(Emphasis Mine)

Since Jesus came, we no longer need the Ark of the Covenant to house the presence of God here on earth. Jesus was called Emmanuel, meaning *"God with us"* (Matthew 1:23). Because of His great sacrifice, He lives in every true believer on earth today. We are now the temple of the living God, and we are the ark of His new covenant.

1 Corinthians 3:16
Know ye not that ye are the temple of God, and that the Spirit of God dwelleth in you?

Everywhere we go, we take Jesus with us. He should be more real to us as believers today than the presence of God was to the

22

children of Israel who had the Ark of the Covenant in the wilderness. He is no longer a God who lives in temples made with man's hands.

Acts 17:24

God that made the world and all things therein, seeing that he is Lord of heaven and earth, dwelleth not in temples made with hands.

God's desire was always to be close to those He loved. It was He who said to the children of Israel in the wilderness:

Exodus 19:5-6

Now therefore, if ye will obey my voice indeed, and keep my covenant, then ye shall be a peculiar treasure unto me above all people: for all the earth is mine: and ye shall be unto me a kingdom of priests, and an holy nation. These are the words which thou shalt speak unto the children of Israel.

But the children of Israel rejected God when He spoke the Ten Commandments audibly from Mt. Sinai. He was revealing Himself to His people, but they preferred to have Moses talk to God for them than to have God speak directly to them. So, Moses became the mediator, the mouthpiece for God. This was not God's original intention with His chosen people. He wanted fellowship, but the people desired distance.

The Ark of the Tabernacle and all that went with it was a substitute for what could have been an Abraham-type relationship with God, one person trusting God through faith, obedience, and love. God was looking for intimacy, but the children of Israel were not interested in such things. They're hearts were still in Egypt. They had left Egypt, but Egypt had not left them.

So, God created a system of worship and sacrifice based on rules and religious acts of service and duty. For their part, the children of Israel throughout history struggled with these rules (beginning with the Ten Commandments) that God had given them to follow. God knew they were not capable of living without breaking those rules, so He provided a temporary sacrificial system, the blood of animals that was used to cover their sins once a year.

> **THE CHILDREN OF ISRAEL THROUGHOUT HISTORY STRUGGLED WITH THESE RULES (BEGINNING WITH THE TEN COMMANDMENTS) THAT GOD HAD GIVEN THEM TO FOLLOW!**

This system was made up of a high priest, other priests, the tabernacle, and the articles in the tabernacle, including the Ark of the Covenant, where the presence of the Lord would dwell. Once a year, the High Priest would take the blood of the sacrifice into the Holy of Holies, to be sprinkled on the Mercy Seat between the two angels. This ritual would cover the sins of the people for the past year.

It was vital that the Ark of the Covenant with the tablets containing the Ten Commandments, a bowl of manna, and the budding rod of Aaron all be in the Ark. It was also on this Ark of the Covenant that the tangible presence of God was to dwell. That sets the scene for what was to come.

> # THE ARK OF THE TABERNACLE AND ALL THAT WENT WITH IT WAS A SUBSTITUTE FOR WHAT COULD HAVE BEEN AN ABRAHAM-TYPE RELATIONSHIP WITH GOD, ONE PERSON TRUSTING GOD THROUGH FAITH, OBEDIENCE, AND LOVE!

CHAPTER 2

THE HISTORY OF THE ARK

After you put into the ark the words of my promise which I will give you, place the throne of mercy on top. I will be above the throne of mercy between the angels whenever I meet with you and give you all my commands for the Israelites.   Exodus 25:21-22, GW

THE ARK IN THE WILDERNESS

God intended the ark to be:

A PLACE FOR MEETING GOD — The longing of the Father was to fellowship with His people as He had with Adam and Eve.

A PLACE TO COMMUNE WITH GOD—This was for those who were set apart and consecrated to God to enter the actual presence of the Almighty, the Creator of the Universe.

The Ark was the conduit to God's power, the evidence of His favor on a people who were chosen by Him because of Abraham, their father. This golden representation of God on earth would also prove to bring the nation of Israel great victories in battle, as the priests carried it and the people marched behind it.

> THE ARK WAS THE CONDUIT TO GOD'S POWER, THE EVIDENCE OF HIS FAVOR ON A PEOPLE WHO WERE CHOSEN BY HIM BECAUSE OF ABRAHAM, THEIR FATHER!

God didn't need their rituals, their ceremony, or their works of ministry. He wanted communion. The Holy of Holies with the Ark carefully placed inside it was a place God could speak to men on earth to give them direction, instruction, and, most of all, fellowship. It was a place to connect with those who were consecrated to Him. He would prove that the children of Israel needed Him to function as a nation, as a people, and as God's chosen children who were separated for His purpose.

Numbers 7:89

And when Moses was gone into the tabernacle of the congregation to speak with him, then he heard the voice of one speaking unto him from off the mercy seat that was upon the ark of testimony, from between the two cherubims: and he spake unto him.

Numbers 9:15-18

And on the day that the tabernacle was reared up the cloud covered the tabernacle, namely, the tent of the testimony: and at even there was upon the tabernacle as it were the appearance of fire, until the morning. So it was alway: the cloud covered it by day, and the appearance of fire by night. And when the cloud was taken up from the tabernacle, then after that the children of Israel journeyed: and in the place where the cloud abode, there the children of Israel pitched their tents. At the commandment of the LORD *the children of Israel journeyed, and at the commandment of the* LORD *they pitched: as long as the cloud abode upon the tabernacle they rested in their tents.*

The glory cloud of God's tangible presence rested on the Ark as a cloud by day and fire by night for all see. God was all about the demonstration of His presence. He wanted everyone to know He was there.

When the cloud and fire moved, the entire congregation was to pack up everything and follow His presence. When He stopped, they also stopped. His presence was always the focal point, the center of everything, while they were on their way to the Promised Land.

THE ARK IN SOLOMON'S TEMPLE

The Ark of the Covenant was kept in a temporary tent called "the Tent of the Congregation" until King Solomon (David's son) built a house for the Lord. His Temple was spectacular in its construction. He went all out and built a magnificent temple to house the Ark of the Covenant in the Holy of Holies. It took four and a half tons of gold to build this temple for the Lord. At today's prices, it would have cost around $278,400,000,000.

> **GOD WAS ALL ABOUT THE DEMONSTRATION OF HIS PRESENCE. HE WANTED EVERYONE TO KNOW HE WAS THERE!**

Here is the Bible account of what happened when this magnificent edifice was dedicated to the Lord:

2 Chronicles 5:2 and 7, and 13-14
Then Solomon assembled the elders of Israel, and all the heads of the tribes,

the chief of the fathers of the children of Israel, unto Jerusalem, to bring up the ark of the covenant of the LORD out of the city of David, which is Zion.

And the priests brought in the ark of the covenant of the LORD unto his place, to the oracle of the house, into the most holy place, even under the wings of the cherubims.

It came even to pass, as the trumpeters and singers were as one, to make one sound to be heard in praising and thanking the LORD; and when they lifted up their voice with the trumpets and cymbals and instruments of musick, and praised the LORD, saying, For he is good; for his mercy endureth for ever: that **then the house was filled with a cloud, even the house of the LORD; so that the priests could not stand to minister by reason of the cloud: for the glory of the LORD had filled the house of God.** (Emphasis Mine)

For four hundred and ten years, Solomon's Temple (also known as the First Temple) housed the Ark of the Covenant with God's presence dwelling in that temple. However, the people of Israel did not always do what God wanted them to do. Many of the kings of Israel were not faithful to obey Him or His commandments. Many prophets were sent to the kings and to the people, urging them to return to the Lord their God and not serve other gods. Their willful disobedience to the Lord brought judgement upon them.

In 587 BC, the Babylonians and their king, King Nebuchadnezzar, seized the city of Jerusalem, destroyed everything in it, and took many of the Jewish people into captivity, all a direct result of their disobedience to God. When this happened, the Ark of the Covenant disappeared from the pages of history and was never mentioned again in the Old Testament.

The Apocrypha states, in 2 Maccabees 2:5, that Jeremiah the prophet hid the Ark in a cave before the Babylonians could capture it and take it away to Babylon. It has never been found.

THE SECOND TEMPLE

After fifty-three years of the Temple in Jerusalem being destroyed, Zerubbabel re-laid the foundations for it. Cyrus, the King of Persia, had allowed the Jews to go back to their holy city and rebuild their Temple in the time of Ezra and Zechariah.

Ezra 3:10-13

And when the builders laid the foundation of the temple of the Lord, they set the priests in their apparel with trumpets, and the Levites the sons of Asaph with cymbals, to praise the Lord, after the ordinance of David king of Israel. And they sang together by course in praising and giving thanks unto the Lord; because he is good, for his mercy endureth for ever toward Israel.

And all the people shouted with a great shout, when they praised the Lord, because the foundation of the house of the Lord was laid. ***But many of the priests and Levites and chief of the*** *fathers, who were ancient men, that had seen the first house, when the foundation of this house was laid before their eyes, wept with a loud voice; and many shouted aloud for joy: so that the people could not discern the noise of the shout of joy from the noise of the weeping of the people: for the people shouted with a loud shout, and the noise was heard afar off.* (Emphasis Mine)

When Zerubbabel, the governor of Judea under the Persians, relaid the foundation of the Temple, the young people rejoiced because of the progress, and the priests and elders who had seen the First Temple wept. These who had seen the First Temple, the one that Solomon had built, knew that the Ark of the Covenant would not be in this Temple as it had been before. They knew that they were settling for a form of religious duty in place of the power and presence of God Himself.

The Ark of the Covenant was never placed in the Second Temple. The Holy of Holies in the Second Temple was an empty chamber. It was without the Ark of the Covenant and the corresponding power of God.

> **THE ARK OF THE COVENANT WAS NEVER PLACED IN THE SECOND TEMPLE. THE HOLY OF HOLIES IN THE SECOND TEMPLE WAS AN EMPTY CHAMBER, WITHOUT THE ARK OF THE COVENANT AND THE CORRESPONDING POWER OF GOD!**

For years the High Priest and the other priests performed their rituals and sacrifices, acting as if everything was normal, but the Ark of the Covenant was not there.

There were three things that were in the Ark that were also now missing in the lives of the children of Israel.

Hebrews 9:3-4

And after the second veil, the tabernacle which is called the Holiest of all; which had the golden censer, and the ark of the covenant overlaid round about with gold, wherein was **the golden pot that had manna, and Aaron's rod that budded, and the tables of the cov- enant.** (Emphasis Mine)

THE TABLETS OF THE LAW (THE TEN COMMANDMENTS)

The tablets of the law were God's reminder to the children of Israel that this law was from Him. God wrote those laws on a tablet of stone, and Moses later rewrote them on another tablet of stone after He had broken the original ones in anger because of the people's disobedience.

Now, because there was no law from God, the priests made their own traditions to become law. When there was no law, there was no schoolmaster to instruct them what was right or what was wrong. The priests and the people lived what they *thought* was right instead of allowing God's moral compass to bring them conviction. Where there is no conviction there is no repentance. It is the law that guides the guilty to repentance and turning back to God.

It can be clearly seen in the Old Testament, after the Second Temple was built, that the leaders and children of Israel were, for the most part, worshiping false gods, living their lives doing what angered and saddened God.

THE ROD OF AARON, WHICH REPRESENTED THE MIRACULOUS

When God chose Aaron to be the High Priest for the children of Israel, He told all the leaders of each tribe to put their rods outside the door of their tents overnight. He said that He would reveal to the children of Israel who He had chosen for this important function. The next morning Aaron's rod had budded and produced almonds. God chose who He wanted as priest with signs and wonders.

Not having the Ark in the Second Temple precluded God from showing up and showing off until the time Jesus appeared. With the absence of the tangible presence of God in their worship, miracles were missing from the Jewish leadership, and the people of God did not experience the powerful God they had heard about in the stories of what He had done in their past.

THE BOWL OF MANNA
(THE NOURISHMENT OF THE LORD)

Because the Ark was missing from their worship, the priest and the people didn't have the bread of life. The manna represented what God gives as nourishment for the soul of those who trust Him.

Manna had been provided for the children of Israel in the desert when they had no other provisions to sustain them. For forty years God provided what they needed, and they had to trust Him day by day. When they gathered manna in the morning, they could only take one day's supply. If they gathered more, the manna would spoil and not be edible. On the day before the Sabbath, they could gather two days' supply so that they could honor the Lord's Day without working. On these occasions, the spoiling did not take place. What a great picture of trusting in God alone for their source of spiritual nourishment!

After the Ark of the Covenant was taken, the children of Israel no longer trusted in the Lord as their spiritual Source. It was all ritual and rules without the relationship that God so desired for His people. By the time Jesus showed up, people were fed up with religion and the leaders of their day. There was a separation between the leaders and the people.

The people saw their spiritual leaders as high and lifted up, not like the common people who were so desiring the Messiah to come. Even more serious, the presence of God was missing from the Holy of Holies, and the people had no idea that the glory had departed. The Second Temple was void of what God wanted for His people.

In 63 BC (before the birth of Jesus), Roman armies seized Jerusalem and the famous and powerful Roman general, Pompey, demanded the privilege of entering the Holy of Holies. When he came out, he said he couldn't understand what all the fuss was about. It was only an empty room. This confirmed the fact that there was no Ark in the Second Temple.

> ### THE JEWISH PEOPLE SAW THEIR SPIRITUAL LEADERS AS HIGH AND LIFTED UP, NOT LIKE THE COMMON PEOPLE WHO WERE SO DESIRING THE MESSIAH TO COME!

As was mentioned many times in the New Testament, Jesus went into the Temple. However, He never stepped foot into the Holy of Holies where the presence of God and the Ark of the Covenant should have been. Jesus, the Messiah, was God with us and had all the rights and authority to go into the Holy of Holies, but He never did.

The Jewish people had settled for:

- The Temple without God's presence
- Religion without the glory
- The works of their rituals, without the atonement (covering for sin)

There was no longer a way for them to commune with God. The fire was gone, and Ichabod (the glory has departed) was written on the wall.

The temple without the Ark was just another building; it held no power of itself. It became a mere meeting place, even though God had designed it to be a place of habitation.

JESUS, THE MESSIAH, WAS GOD WITH US AND HAD ALL THE RIGHTS AND AUTHORITY TO GO INTO THE HOLY OF HOLIES, BUT HE NEVER DID!

CHAPTER 3

THE CONDITION OF
THE CHURCH TODAY

Because thou sayest, I am rich, and increased with goods, and have need of nothing; and knowest not that thou art wretched, and miserable, and poor, and blind, and naked: I counsel thee to buy of me gold tried in the fire, that thou mayest be rich; and white raiment, that thou mayest be clothed, and that the shame of thy nakedness do not appear; and anoint thine eyes with eyesalve, that thou mayest see. Revelation 3:17-18

We can learn from the mistakes of past generations. As we look at how the children of Israel treated the most holy things of the Lord, we can see patterns and likenesses of how they followed ritual over relationship, rules over intimacy, and separation over fellowship with God. We can also see that, all along, God was in pursuit of His people.

If we look hard enough, we can see the church of today repeating the same mistakes the children of Israel made. We can also see what happens when you reject what God has provided for you through His grace and lovingkindness. When Israel rejected God, judgement was imminent.

It appears that many churches today are no different than the children of Israel. Many have substituted the fake for the real, the mundane for the glory, and the ability to draw a crowd for the real power of God.

Where are those who weep? Have we forgotten what it was like to experience the tangible presence of God showing up in our gatherings? Have we forgotten when healings and miracles were second nature to us, when God's presence was so real that it would transform the worst of sinners?

Do you remember when God was so real to you that you couldn't move for hours because the glory was so strong? Or how about when you just couldn't stop crying, and you knew that God was changing you through the experience?

> **WHEN ISRAEL REJECTED GOD,
> JUDGEMENT WAS IMMINENT!**

Those older people at the dedication of the foundations of the Second Temple had seen the things God did and knew what it was like to have Him in the house. They knew the cost of losing what once was held dear to their hearts.

> **MANY CHURCHES HAVE SUBSTITUTED
> THE FAKE FOR THE REAL, THE MUNDANE FOR
> THE GLORY, AND THE ABILITY TO DRAW A
> CROWD FOR THE REAL POWER OF GOD!**

There are many today who have experienced the glory, the wonder, and the manifest presence of the Lord, and they long for meetings that will ignite in them once again the passion that only the presence of God can bring. There is also a new generation being drawn into churches today that has never experienced what it is like to be convicted, to have a brokenness that transforms a person and their lifestyle. They have only been in the feel-good type of service with professional-sounding music, light shows, funny antidotes, and powerless proclamations. They have never seen miracles, healings, or the freedom that only being in the presence of God can bring. The perfectly-timed experiences of today's churches rarely allows the Holy Spirit to do what He wants to do in the hearts of hungry and seeking believers.

When the Ark was no longer present, the people were not afraid to enter the Holy of Holies. Because God was no longer present, the fear of the Lord that had once resonated throughout the whole congregation, was now diminished.

Have you ever wondered why the fear of the Lord and repentance are no longer subjects to be preached about in most large sanctuaries filled with masses of believers today or why most pastors in our country no longer preach about the sin in the culture around us?

Have you ever left a church service feeling that something was missing? Oh, yes, you had been thoroughly entertained, but it all left a void on the inside of you, leaving your spirit longing for a move of God. If you have felt this need, then you have become a part of the last-days army that God wants to raise up. He is placing a deep hunger in the hearts of His true people. He that hath an ear to hear will listen and obey the tugging of the Lord for more.

When believers have had enough of mundane one-hour services, only then will they begin to pursue the true manifest presence of God. That is when God will show up, and everything will change.

> **HE THAT HATH AN EAR TO HEAR WILL LISTEN AND OBEY THE TUGGING OF THE LORD FOR MORE!**

When God really shows up, no one wants to leave. I have seen this kind of move of God. I remember when there were lines outside the sanctuary that just went on and on. People were waiting for eight hours just to get in to experience a true life-changing move of God. What most churches have to offer today, in comparison, is just smoke and mirrors.

> **WHEN GOD REALLY SHOWS UP, NO ONE WANTS TO LEAVE!**

So, what did the Second Temple priests do on Yom Kippur when they were to offer up blood on the Mercy Seat of the Ark? They laid the blood where the Ark should have been, on the flat stone that was for the foundation of the Ark, thinking that the foundation of the Ark was probably just as good as the Ark itself. But nothing should keep us from pursuing intimacy with God and His manifest presence.

The priests of the Second Temple offered up the blood of the sacrifices, even though the foundation did not have a Mercy Seat, nor did it have God's presence that should have dwelt between the two cherubim.

William Booth, Founder of the Salvation Army, said:

> *I consider that the chief dangers which confront the coming century will be… religion without the Holy Ghost, Christianity without Christ, forgiveness without repentance, salvation without regeneration, politics without God and heaven without hell.*[1]

As you can see, William Booth was prophetic.

---

1. https://www.newlifepublishing.co.uk/articles/william-booths-army-of-blood-and-fire/#:~:text=%E2%80%9CI%20consider%20that%20the%20chief,%2C%20and%20heaven%20without%20hell.%E2%80%9D

> **I** CONSIDER THAT THE CHIEF
> DANGERS WHICH CONFRONT THE
> COMING CENTURY WILL BE...
> RELIGION WITHOUT THE HOLY GHOST,
> CHRISTIANITY WITHOUT CHRIST,
> FORGIVENESS WITHOUT REPENTANCE,
> SALVATION WITHOUT REGENERATION,
> POLITICS WITHOUT GOD,
> AND HEAVEN WITHOUT HELL.
> — WILLIAM BOOTH

CHAPTER 4

ACCEPT NO SUBSTITUTES

I beseech you therefore, brethren, by the mercies of God, that ye present your bodies a living sacrifice, holy, acceptable unto God, which is your reasonable service. And be not conformed to this world: but be ye transformed by the renewing of your mind, that ye may prove what is that good, and acceptable, and perfect, will of God.   Romans 12:1-2

So, what do we do if we have substituted lifeless, religious acts of service, light shows, funny antidotes, and sermons that entertain for the tangible presence of God and bringing much needed power, healing, miracles, conviction, and direction to the Body of

Christ and to those who are seekers? **You put on a show.** You make the people think that what they are experiencing is just as good as God's best for them. You attempt to show them that they don't need the presence of God to offer themselves as a living sacrifice.

Meanwhile you allow them to think God is pleased with all they are doing for Him. It must be God. Look at how many people are attending! People are pleased and have nothing but good things to say about the preaching, the worship, the activities, the ministry. The church has become a magnet for self-absorbed seekers who are looking for a place of acceptance and freedom to continue in the culture and lifestyle they are accustomed to because of the world around them.

After I had watched about ten minutes of a Christian awards show one night, I asked my wife, "Do you feel the anointing?"

"No," she said.

I was appalled to think that the Body of Christ has substituted worldly, gaudy entertainment and, with it, its adoring fans and half-hearted artists for God's tangible presence and His glory. When you are dancing like the world and acting like the world, you must be part of the world. Where was the anointing that breaks the yokes and bondages of sin, the anointing that we, as a nation, so desperately need right now? It seemed like the church was celebrating mediocrity while ignoring the elephant in the room. There was no demonstration of supernatural power that would transform the listeners.

We might be able to fool people, but we can't fool God. He knows that what we are doing is just a substitute for what He has in store for the last-days church.

John 1:10, TPT
He entered into the very world he created, yet the world was unaware.

When Jesus (the Word, God with Us, the Son of God) came on the scene more than two thousand years ago, He didn't chose to come in an expensive building and He wasn't introduced with a grand light show. There was no pomp and splendor announcing the King of Kings and the Lord of Lords to the world.

> **WE MIGHT BE ABLE TO FOOL PEOPLE, BUT WE CAN'T FOOL GOD. HE KNOWS THAT WHAT WE ARE DOING IS JUST A SUBSTITUTE FOR WHAT HE HAS IN STORE FOR THE LAST-DAYS CHURCH!**

Jesus entered the scene almost five hundred years after the Ark of the Covenant was no longer of importance to God's people. At that time, the religious leaders thought they had it all figured out. They had been so long without God's tangible presence that they were used to not having Him around.

Once you have become accustomed to not having the cloud of God's glory, then the fire doesn't seem to be all that important either. Today, as a church, we have gotten used to doing the work of God without the presence of God.

Oh, we know how to have church. We have figured out how to draw a crowd, how to keep them coming, and how to raise funds for things that we know will attract them to us.

> **TODAY, AS A CHURCH, WE HAVE GOTTEN USED TO DOING THE WORK OF GOD WITHOUT THE PRESENCE OF GOD.**

In Jesus' day, the Jews had figured out how to use the Torah (the Law), their garments, and their rituals to make them look godly without God. At the same time, they were stealing from the people and controlling the masses, and yet they really felt good about themselves. After all, they were religiously faithful to the teachings of Moses. But they had forgotten that Moses received the Law while being in the presence of Almighty God on Mount Sinai.

Jesus said:

Luke 12:2, TPT
Everything hidden and covered up will soon be exposed.

When Jesus took His last breath on the cross, something happened:

Matthew 27:51
And, behold, the veil of the temple was rent in twain from the top to the bottom; and the earth did quake.

> **THEY HAD FORGOTTEN THAT MOSES RECEIVED THE LAW WHILE BEING IN THE PRESENCE OF ALMIGHTY GOD ON MOUNT SINAI!**

It has been taught that God was letting His glory out when the Temple curtain was torn. Others have said it meant that we can come into the Holy of Holies because God tore the curtain for us. What really happened?

It was in that moment that the lie was exposed. The priests could no longer hide the fact that the glory had long since departed. There was no Ark, and the Holy of Holies was empty. However, Jesus (God Himself) was on earth, right in front of them, without a veil to separate, and He was God in the flesh. They missed it, refusing to acknowledge that their religion was an empty ritual.

The one true Messiah had come, and they had killed Him. He had came in compassion and wisdom, and they had rejected Him. He had told them that He was the One, but they had too much to lose to accept it. They would have lost all of what was precious to them—prestige, money, power, and their audience. If they had counted it all as dung like the apostle Paul did, they would have seen clearly. But they were blinded, deceived, and angry.

> **IT WAS IN THAT MOMENT THAT THE LIE WAS EXPOSED!**

When you teach lies, you have to believe them yourself. You make up excuses because you don't need God's presence or His glory. So, you learn to manipulate, to be more charismatic, to appeal to people's emotions, to make them laugh. This show becomes a substitute for God Himself. At times, it is faking what God intended to be very real. Why would God want to show up in the midst of all that? So, He doesn't.

There are no miracles, so we have to come up with the next best thing. Void of any trace of true anointing, we have endless activity with no power, words with no authority, preaching with man's wisdom and with no actual demonstration of the power of God to heal or set free those who are bound by demon spirits. In the process, we are disregarding the Holy Spirit and His gifts.

> **WHY WOULD GOD WANT TO SHOW UP IN THE MIDST OF ALL THAT? SO, HE DOESN'T.**

This is what was going on when Jesus showed up. He exposed the lies, and they killed Him for it. But because of Jesus, no longer will humanity have to depend on religious leaders to offer the blood of sheep for the forgiveness of their sins. The religious acts, rituals, and formulas are no longer needed to take the place of God in the hearts, minds, and souls of mankind. We are now called to a relationship with a loving God. He wants us to long for Him, to pursue Him, and to abide in Him.

John 15:4-8

Abide in me, and I in you. As the branch cannot bear fruit of itself, except it abide in the vine; no more can ye, except ye abide in me.

I am the vine, ye are the branches: He that abideth in me, and I in him, the same bringeth forth much fruit: for without me ye can do nothing. If a man abide not in me, he is cast forth as a branch, and is withered; and men gather them, and cast them into the fire, and they are burned. If ye abide in me, and my words abide in you, ye shall ask

*what ye will, and it shall be done unto
you. Herein is my Father glorified, that
ye bear much fruit; so shall ye be my
disciples.*

If we do not abide in Jesus, we are cast forth
as a branch is thrown into a fire. We don't
have to put on a show for Him. He just wants
our complete devotion to Him. A show has
always been the way to draw a crowd. But
is Christianity about drawing a crowd, or is
it about wanting God in our midst?

**WE ARE NOW CALLED TO A RELATIONSHIP
WITH A LOVING GOD. HE WANTS US TO LONG FOR
HIM, TO PURSUE HIM, AND TO ABIDE IN HIM!**

When the Body of Christ decides to make it
all about Jesus and what He wants us to do,
everything will change. Jesus loves to show
up and show off when He is welcomed.

The Spirit of God is always checking the
motives of the hearts of His people when

they gather together. Why are we doing what we're doing? And who are we doing it for? What is the Holy Spirit looking for? He is looking for vessels that are pure and hungry for more of God. He is looking for those who have laid it all down for Jesus.

> **IF WE DO NOT ABIDE IN JESUS,**
> **WE ARE CAST FORTH AS A BRANCH**
> **IS THROWN INTO A FIRE!**

Luke 9:23-26,TPT

Jesus said to all of his followers, "If you truly desire to be my disciple, you must disown your life completely, embrace my cross as your own, and surrender to my ways. For if you choose self-sacrifice, giving up your lives for my glory, you will embark on a discovery of more and more of true life. But if you choose to keep your lives for yourselves, you will lose what you try to keep. Even if you gained all the wealth and power of this world, everything it could offer you, yet lost your soul in the process, what good is that? So why then are you ashamed of being my disciple? Are you ashamed of the revelation-truth I give to you? I, the Son of Man, will one day return in my radiant brightness, with the holy angels and in the splendor and majesty of my Father, and I will be ashamed of all who are ashamed of me.

WHY ARE WE DOING WHAT WE'RE DOING? AND WHO ARE WE DOING IT FOR?

Once you have seen the real, felt the real, and experienced the real, the real tangible presence of God, you will no longer settle for the fake, and nothing that people try to do to take the place of God will satisfy you. Why? Because His presence has changed you. It has marked you for life. It has been forever embedded in you. You know that's what Heaven will be like.

God's presence changes our perspective. His glory brings a reverence and a holy fear, an awe and wonder at just how powerful, yet loving our God really is.

Why would I want the fake when I can have the real thing? Why should I accept anything less than what God wants to give me? He wants me to have *Him*. He wants me to know Him, commune with Him, be instructed by Him. He wants me to know that He is there. This eternal, loving, fearful, holy God wants to have a real relationship with me.

> IS CHRISTIANITY ABOUT DRAWING A CROWD, OR IS IT ABOUT WANTING GOD IN OUR MIDST?

But what if you have never known what it's like to commune with this awesome God and never seen or felt the effects of His glory? What if you've never had a holy visitation? What if you have only seen the fake or been worked up by emotions because the preacher was skillful with words and knew how to push the right buttons or the worship team was able to play and sing the song that connected with you best? Today's church has extremely skillful musicians and singers who hit every note with perfection. Instead of the awe and wonder of God showing up, you have only experienced the lights and fog machines that make you feel like something is happening in the house. But it's all just smoke and mirrors, hiding the fact that God has been substituted by a show.

> **WHY WOULD I WANT THE FAKE WHEN I CAN HAVE THE REAL THING? WHY SHOULD I ACCEPT ANYTHING LESS THAN WHAT GOD WANTS TO GIVE ME?**

Does this all leave the congregation excited but not changed, thrilled but not having the fear of God, desperate and disillusioned because it was never real, wondering if this is all that God has to offer? How can we be led by the Spirit if we have exempted, controlled, and completely disregarded the Spirit Himself?

Mario Murillo, a popular minister, has said: "All the glittering fool's gold and false success of Christian empires can only be exposed if God reveals to us what we might have had if we had obeyed the Holy Spirit."

This is one of the biggest deceptions in the church today. We, as a body of believers, are now seeing the results of these lies that the enemy has fooled us with.

Let us, as the beloved of the Lord, never settle for the fake glory or the unsatisfying lies of the enemy. Wanting all that He has for His church, may we pursue Jesus in all of His glory and splendor, leaving no stone unturned until we see Him as He is. I will not settle for a show. I want Jesus!

> # HOW CAN WE BE LED BY THE SPIRIT IF WE HAVE EXEMPTED, CONTROLLED, AND COMPLETELY DISREGARDED THE SPIRIT HIMSELF?

I WILL NOT SETTLE FOR A SHOW! I WANT JESUS!

CHAPTER 5

BROKEN BY THE CHURCH

Behold, I send you forth as sheep in the
midst of wolves: be ye therefore wise as
serpents, and harmless as doves.

Matthew 10:16

You may be wondering how I can be so
outspoken when it comes to the condition
of the church today? How can I say these
things that will surely offend or upset the
establishment and movements that I feel
are destroying the mindset of the church in
these last days? The answer is that I am writing these things from experience. I know
what happens to pastors who fight against
the Jezebel spirits nonstop in their congrega-
tions. I also know how it feels to experience

the tangible presence of God, with people being healed, set free, and delivered on a regular basis.

I have been talked bad about because of what God was doing in our church services and been rejected by my peers for allowing the Holy Spirit to move however He wanted to throughout our congregation. I have been considered radical by many.

This experience, this move of God, was not just in the church I pastored, but this experience was personal. God had visited me, and I was forever changed. I had encountered the living God in such a way that transformed my way of thinking and my way of doing ministry.

My experience brought me into a fellowship that I had desired for a very long time. For many years I prayed for real revival, I preached it, taught it, and lived in it. What an awesome transformation the Holy Spirit made in my own life!

One night the Lord woke me up with these words, "rivers, rivers, rivers." I felt God's presence so strong that it was shaking me.

He was screaming those words to me. Then I saw, in a vision, all the bayous of Louisiana connecting to other waterways and eventually connecting to the Mississippi River, then the Mississippi connecting to every other waterway in the United States.

RIVERS!

RIVERS!

RIVERS!

God spoke to me, "I will use the bayous of Louisiana as a conduit for the Spirit of God to be poured out all over your nation." He gave me directions about what to do and how to do it.

I began to do all that the Spirit was instructing me. Revival was changing hearts and lives, and I wanted it to continue forever. Sadly, however, people became weary, and prayer began to diminish in the church. What you gain through prayer must be maintained through prayer!

Revival was no longer the focus in the hearts of those who had once contended for the faith. Personally, through the process of this fantastic move of God that lasted about six months, I was a different person. I longed for God's presence and wanted more of Him. He began a work in me in a way that I am still processing today in my own life and ministry.

> **WHAT YOU GAIN THROUGH PRAYER MUST BE MAINTAINED THROUGH PRAYER!**

I eventually moved on by the leading of the Lord to pastor a church in another state, and God was doing some great things in that church. The youth and children were being touched, and the Lord was bringing in drug addicts from a nearby mountain area. Whole families were coming to the Lord, families that had been devastated by the drug culture that had bound them for many years. We were seeing growth because of another move of God, but this move of God was touching the world, and we were seeing actual life transformation.

One year after becoming the pastor of this church, we were up for a vote to see if we would continue to be the pastor. We were very surprised to learn that a group of older members who had stopped attending were not happy with the type of people now coming into their church, and so they voted us out.

My wife and I, along with our youngest son, were devastated by this decision. We had been sure that God had called us there. It literally took us months to recover from this rejection, being cast aside in this way. But God saw us through this hard time and brought healing and restoration to us.

We were invited to try out for a church in another state that eventually accepted us as their senior pastors. There we felt wanted and loved again. I pressed into God and regained the heart of the revival that seemed to have diminished because of my bad experiences with the prior church.

We were in that church for a year before the dreaded vote was taken, once again, to see if the people wanted us to stay as their pastors. To our surprise, we were again voted out. I learned that the church had gone through five pastors before me, voting each of them out in turn. We were their sixth pastor in seven years.

We were so traumatized by this turn of events that we decided to pull back and just attend a large local church in our area to find comfort and restoration from the recent blows of the enemy. We had never been part of such a large church before, and we seemed to just blend into the crowd. We didn't know anyone there, and for months we just sat back and were not responsible for anything.

Through all of this, we became disillusioned by the condition of the church and didn't understand what God was doing. Personally, I was truly broken by the church.

It took a while, but I slowly began to try to connect and had the hope of becoming a leader in this church that seemed to have it all together. Maybe I could learn something from them. Then I learned that to become a leader in the church, you had to attend their discipleship process and "learn their culture" before you could do anything in the church.

> **I LEARNED THAT THE CHURCH HAD GONE THROUGH FIVE PASTORS BEFORE ME, VOTING EACH OF THEM OUT IN TURN!**

I had no idea what they were talking about, and it really upset me to have to go to classes that were for beginners, when I had already pastored full-time for eleven years.

I began to search for another church to pastor, wanting to fulfill the call of God on my life. My wife and son were very understanding, and together we decided to try out for a church an hour away that needed a pastor.

We were accepted as their pastors and had great hopes for God to move as He had done in the past. However, it didn't take long to see that there were real problems in this church. Throughout the coming months we were in a real battle that proved to be a great challenge to us all.

Our son eventually connected with some of the youth there, and we pressed through and made some necessary changes to the way things were being done. Eventually, things began to go great. We did many much-needed repairs to the church, we reorganized the ministries to work more effectively, and we were beginning to reach out into the community to make a difference.

When we had been there one year, the church's annual business meeting was coming up. Surely the progress, the hard work we were doing, and the potential for growth because of the planned outreaches coming up would prove to secure our place to continue as their pastors for the future ... or so we thought. Instead, they, too, voted us out.

I couldn't believe it. My son was devastated, my wife was very discouraged, and I was a wreck. I had again been broken by the church. The past move of God in my life now seemed to be a distant memory. It may have been a hope for the future, but at that moment, I couldn't feel God's presence, I had no power, and I was lost in a sea of pain. It took all that I had to go back to the large church that we had been attending before.

I know what it's like to have the tangible, glorious presence of God, see signs and wonders, and operate in the gifts of the Spirit, watching people's lives being transformed right before my eyes, but I have also tasted the bitter cup of rejection from the existing church. I know what it is like to pour yourself into people, give them your all and be the shepherd God has called you to be to them, only to be discarded in the end. That does a number on you.

There is a real fear in pastors today that breeds caution to preach against sin or ruffle the feathers of those in the church who are compromising. With all the pressures that are looming from dealing with people who are not consecrated to live what they say they believe, pastors feel the need to sugar-coat the message of the cross.

> **I KNOW WHAT IT'S LIKE TO HAVE THE TANGIBLE, GLORIOUS PRESENCE OF GOD, SEE SIGNS AND WONDERS, AND OPERATE IN THE GIFTS OF THE SPIRIT, WATCHING PEOPLE'S LIVES BEING TRANSFORMED RIGHT BEFORE MY EYES, BUT I HAVE ALSO TASTED THE BITTER CUP OF REJECTION FROM THE EXISTING CHURCH!**

No wonder they never get around to addressing the lies of our current culture! The result is that the culture of the world is causing many believers to decline spiritually and succumb to darkness, while the church refuses to deal with this situation from the pulpit.

The last-days church is called to take back territory from the enemy and to disciple believers and prepare them to be a holy church without spot or wrinkle. Just before the coming of the Lord, the Body of Christ should not be living in compromise or be coddled by their leaders to fail to live their best life. We are soldiers, and we should be preparing to do battle against the enemy that is holding the masses captive all around us.

However, when true pastors, prophets, teachers, evangelists, and apostles preach the Gospel that John the Baptist preached, Jesus proclaimed and lived, and the disciples wrote about in the Word of God, people get offended. They don't want to be corrected. They want to continue living in sin and still be able to call themselves Christians. They want to go to church and then feel like they have done their duty for the week.

When Jesus called His disciples, they were told to follow Him. They had to leave everything and surrender to whatever He was doing. That is what it means to be a disciple of Jesus. If leaders in the church require anything of most members of the church today, they pick up and leave. Their goal is to find a church down the road that lets them do what they want and still be called a Christian. I would not want to be a leader in that type of church on Judgement Day.

> **WHEN TRUE PASTORS, PROPHETS, TEACHERS, EVANGELISTS, AND APOSTLES PREACH THE GOSPEL THAT JOHN THE BAPTIST PREACHED, JESUS PROCLAIMED AND LIVED, AND THE DISCIPLES WROTE ABOUT IN THE WORD OF GOD, PEOPLE GET OFFENDED!**

There are many reasons why the church body is looking for a safe place to land, why the Body of Christ is filling churches that don't preach the whole Gospel, why believers want their ears to be tickled instead of them being challenged to be more like Jesus. People use going to church as a means to settle their conscience, while living a lie the rest of the week. But the question to ask is this: are they truly committed to becoming a disciplined learner and follower of the Lord and Savior, Jesus Christ?

No wonder pastors are sugar-coating the message of the cross and avoiding mention of discipline, holiness, and repentance! This makes it easier not to ruffle the feathers of those they are trying to keep in their churches. No one likes conflict, so they choose not to expose the culture that is destroying our nation. As a pastor, we must make sure the bills are paid and salaries are met each week. If we preach the wrong message, some people may leave, abandoning us without a word of explanation, and others will stir up a hornet's nest within.

The Bible never said it would be easy to be a pastor. As a matter of fact, pastors have one of the most difficult jobs on the planet. I have learned this for myself. My greatest mistake in these times of rejection was that I didn't shake the dust off my feet immediately.

Matthew 10:14

And whosoever shall not receive you, nor hear your words, when ye depart out of that house or city, shake off the dust of your feet.

This was a terrible mistake on my part. The root of rejection was deep, it brought me much pain, and kept me from God's best in my life for many years. As a matter of fact, rejection led me to seek out a church that I thought would heal my wounds and help me with the pain. I had no idea that this church had developed a culture that brought in many but had hardly any passion for the presence of God.

IF WE PREACH THE WRONG MESSAGE, SOME PEOPLE MAY LEAVE, ABANDONING US WITHOUT A WORD OF EXPLANATION, AND OTHERS WILL STIR UP A HORNET'S NEST WITHIN!

At first, the welcoming atmosphere in the church was very appealing to me. I needed healing for my brokenness, and my family needed a safe place to land. I was comforted there and the conflicts in the past three churches I had pastored began diminishing in my mind. I had no idea that this was a trap of the enemy.

Because I had experienced revival and the manifest presence of God in my life, these memories were always there in the depths of my spirit, reminding me that there was more. There were times when I would pursue God and begin to see a renewed spiritual hunger in my life, but this would create sparks with those I connected with in the Body of Christ. I knew that I was to be a carrier of revival, and I would see a glimmer of hope for a new move of God. But invariably, when this happened, there was always pushback from the church leadership team.

At one point, things looked very hopeful. The senior pastor asked my wife and me to pastor a satellite church they were starting in a town about forty-five minutes away. We agreed and were very excited to finally be able to do what we felt God wanted us to do as part of this hugely successful church family.

Then, two weeks went by and we heard through the grapevine that the new church had been given to someone else to pastor. There was not a word to us from the pastor, who had told us two weeks before that we would be the pastors of this new work. When he did speak to us about it, it was to ask if we would lead the worship for the new church, to help get it started and running well. We had no idea what we had done to change his mind.

I handled this fourth rejection a lot better than the other three. This time I refused to let rejection wound me. This event and how I handled it helped to establish me at the large church, allowing me to connect in a greater way to the senior pastor and all the other pastors. It seemed that I was finally being accepted into their culture.

Along with our acceptance as a part of this large, successful church, I was pursuing the presence of God and wanting to see a move of God in my own circles of influence. However, it seemed that I could not have both worlds. There seemed to be two kingdoms at work there. They were 1). The revival culture that was conceived as "messing up our plans and programs," and 2). The culture of the church model that never ruffled the feathers of the believers or challenged them to go deeper. These two forces were always in opposition to one another.

> **THESE TWO FORCES WERE ALWAYS IN OPPOSITION TO ONE ANOTHER!**

I thought that things would change, that the leadership would eventually recognize the need for the deeper things of God. I was even thinking that I might one day become a pastor under their leadership, and God would pour out His Spirit as before. However, after about six years of pursuing this dream, the Lord spoke to me and said, "Why are you doing what you're doing? Check your motives."

I took a month off from all ministry duties to spend time in fasting and praying about what God was telling me, and in the process I realized that my motives had not been pure. I was pursuing ministry for the wrong reasons.

"WHY ARE YOU DOING WHAT YOU ARE DOING? CHECK YOUR MOTIVES."

I had also not dealt with the rejection as I should have and was still trying to minister out of hurt for what had happened in the past. I realized that the frustration I was feeling came from not being where God wanted me to be spiritually. I was not in pursuit of God's presence; I was in pursuit of success. I wanted to be part of a "successful church" because of the root of rejection that had not been healed in me. I wanted to see the numbers, but at the same time, experience the glory I had experienced in revival, and the two didn't go together.

When we see ministries growing in numbers, we tend to take notice and try to get what they have. This requires that we do what they are doing. It is what the mega-churches call "culture." It is a method, a process, steps that guarantee success, and it reduces the work of the ministry to formulas and processes. The problem with this is: the Kingdom of God is not built upon culture; it is built upon the Rock, which is Jesus and His power.

The cross always was and still is a place to die to self. The message of the true Gospel is that through repentance we are saved. Jesus gave His commission to the church, it was: "Go and preach the Gospel," not to draw the lost into the church with programs, lights, and funny sermons. The Kingdom is the power of the Holy Spirit working in the church, with signs and wonders following, healings, miracles, and the gifts of the Spirit in operation.

Paul wrote to the believers in Corinth:

1 Corinthians 2:1-4
And I, brethren, when I came to you, came not with excellency of speech or

of wisdom, declaring unto you the testimony of God. For I determined not to know anything among you, save Jesus Christ, and him crucified. And I was with you in weakness, and in fear, and in much trembling. And my speech and my preaching was not with enticing words of man's wisdom, but in demonstration of the Spirit and of power.

Let it never be said that we are willing to compromise what Jesus paid such a great price for just for the sake of success through numbers.

As I later looked back on my many mistakes in this period in my life, I realized that I had to be healed of rejection. It had caused me to make some wrong choices in the direction of my life and ministry. Rejection caused me great pain, when all I had to do was to dust off my feet and give it all to Jesus, trusting that He knew best and would take care of me in all the storms of life. It wasn't me people were rejecting; it was God. I took on offence that I was not intended to carry.

All that pain was so unnecessary, and now six years of my life seemed to have been wasted going in circles. I had fallen for the trap of the enemy. But God is faithful and always seems to make a way to get us back on track. If these events had not happened as they did, I would not have been able to understand this great battle that the church is facing in these last days.

LET IT NEVER BE SAID THAT WE ARE WILLING TO COMPROMISE WHAT JESUS PAID SUCH A GREAT PRICE FOR JUST FOR THE SAKE OF SUCCESS THROUGH NUMBERS!

I can now see with clear vision the traps that the enemy is placing in front of us all right now. My prayer is that the pain of this battle that I fought will bring many to wake up and pursue the glory of God's presence in such a way that they will become prepared to be part of the last-days army that God will use in a great way.

It was the manifest presence of the Lord that healed me. I needed Him more than I needed ministry. My deception came because ministry became my focus and success was my priority. I was looking for my purpose and didn't realize that without Jesus and His wisdom, my purpose would never be fulfilled.

> **IT WASN'T ME PEOPLE WERE REJECTING; IT WAS GOD. I TOOK ON AN OFFENCE THAT I WAS NOT INTENDED TO CARRY!**

How easily we get pulled away from the true prize! How vain we can get when we think we can make things happen on our own, when all along we are miserable because we had left wisdom's guiding hand along the way! You can't take back the time wasted pursuing your own dream through your own efforts.

I failed to realized what this would do to my family. It is heartbreaking to know that the pain my wife and son were going through was really my fault. It was my ambition that led me to choose ministry over their wellbeing, all the time thinking that I was doing the right thing.

I am so thankful for the mercy and grace of the Lord on my behalf. He allowed me to hit bottom spiritually, and this gave me a wake-up call. I am thankful that He is the Redeemer of time and that He forgives and redeems us when we go our own way.

I CAN NOW SEE WITH CLEAR VISION THE TRAPS THAT THE ENEMY IS PLACING IN FRONT OF US ALL RIGHT NOW. MY PRAYER IS THAT THE PAIN OF THIS BATTLE THAT I FOUGHT WILL BRING MANY TO WAKE UP AND PURSUE THE GLORY OF GOD'S PRESENCE IN SUCH A WAY THAT THEY WILL BECOME PREPARED TO BE PART OF THE LAST-DAYS ARMY THAT GOD WILL USE IN A GREAT WAY!

CHAPTER 6

THE GENUINE PURSUIT OF GOD

Now, therefore, you are no longer strangers and foreigners, but fellow citizens with the saints and members of the household of God, having been built on the foundation of the apostles and prophets, Jesus Christ Himself being the chief cornerstone, in whom the whole building, being fitted together, grows into a holy temple in the Lord, in whom you also are being built together for a dwelling place of God in the Spirit. Ephesians 2:19-22, NKJV

As the Body of Christ, we are now known as the dwelling place of God Himself. His Spirit dwells in us. The individual believer, as a member of the Body of Christ, has taken the place of the Holy of Holies on earth.

Colossians 1:26-27

*Even the mystery which hath been hid from ages and from generations, but now is made manifest to his saints: to whom God would make known what is the riches of the glory of this mystery among the Gentiles; **Christ in you the hope of glory.*** (Emphasis Mine)

Jesus was such a good example of what the church today should look like. He carried the anointing of the Holy Spirit wherever He went. He was filled with the Spirit and baptized in power when He came out of the wilderness after forty days of fasting.

Most of Jesus' ministry was outside the four walls of a building. Yes, He went to the Temple and the synagogues. He gathered to teach His disciples in many different places throughout the time of His ministry. He was God in the flesh with power and authority over sickness, disease, and demons everywhere He went.

With authority, Jesus commanded the winds and the seas to obey Him. He even conquered death by raising the dead. This Jesus was filled with the glory of the Father and led by the Spirit. He only did what He saw the Father do.

John 14:12-17, CEV

I tell you for certain that if you have faith in me, you will do the same things that I am doing. You will do even greater things, now that I am going back to the Father. Ask me, and I will do whatever you ask. This way the Son will bring honor to the Father. I will do whatever you ask me to do.

Jesus said to his disciples: If you love me, you will do as I command. Then I will ask the Father to send you the Holy Spirit who will help you and always be with you. The Spirit will show you what is true. The people of this world cannot accept the Spirit, because they don't see or know him. But you know the Spirit, who is with you and will keep on living in you.

John 14:26

> *But the Comforter, which is the Holy Ghost, whom the Father will send in my name, he shall teach you all things, and bring all things to your remembrance, whatsoever I have said unto you.*

Yes, we are the Ark of God's presence today. His Spirit now dwells in us. Everywhere we go, we take God with us. The power that Jesus had is available to every believer alive today.

WE ARE THE ARK OF THE GOD'S PRESENCE TODAY!

Before He was lifted back up into Heaven, Jesus told His disciples to wait for the promised Holy Spirit. He did not tell them, "When I leave you today, go and preach the Gospel and pray for the sick." He said nothing about ministry. He wanted them to know that the most important thing they could do for the Kingdom's advancement was to wait for the Holy Spirit. When He had come, they would be endued with power from on high to be His witnesses.

They had been with Jesus for three and a half years. They had heard the sermons He preached and seen the miracles and healings He did. At times, Jesus had even given them authority to go themselves, and God used them in a powerful way with signs and wonders following. With all that training and the demonstration right before their eyes, they were still not ready to go and preach the Gospel. These disciples needed the baptism in the Holy Spirit before they could even begin to do what God wanted them to do.

That is how important it is to be overflowing with the power and manifest presence of God before we can be effective in our world. It was the power and presence of God that the disciples needed to change their world, and it the power and presence of God that is needed to change our world today.

The continual pursuit of the presence of God and the leading of the Spirit in our lives and ministries is just as vital and important today as it was when the church started in the book of Acts. There is no substitute for the power and demonstration of the Spirit of God in our churches today.

Putting on a good show doesn't change the hearts of those who are lost and destitute. Sin cannot be eradicated in the hearts of the lost by making people feel good or tickling their ears. It is the power of the cross and the blood of Jesus that saves the sin-sick soul when they truly repent, being convicted by a true presentation of the Gospel of Jesus Christ. It is the presence of a holy God that brings conviction that will change the hard heart.

> **THESE DISCIPLES NEEDED THE BAPTISM IN THE HOLY SPIRIT BEFORE THEY COULD EVEN BEGIN TO DO WHAT GOD WANTED THEM TO DO!**

God will put on His own show when we pursue Him. When we are filled to overflowing by the Spirit of God because we have been in His presence, He shows up and shows off. Miracles happen when God is in the house. People get healed, and the gifts of the Spirit are in operation. God wants to demonstrate how much He loves it when a holy people call out to a holy God in pure submission and dedication to His will.

The leadership and the believers in the book of Acts didn't just preach the Word; they had the demonstration of power, miracles, and healing in operation, and this confirmed the Word they were preaching. They were united in the Temple and going from house to house eating and fellowshipping together. The numbers increased, and people were being changed because God was moving. It was pure, it was sweet, and it was focused on Jesus.

Acts 2:42-47

And they continued stedfastly in the apostles' doctrine and fellowship, and in breaking of bread, and in prayers. And fear came upon every soul: and many wonders and signs were done by the apostles.

And all that believed were together, and had all things common; and sold their possessions and goods, and parted them to all men, as every man had need. And they, continuing daily with one accord in the temple, and breaking bread from house to house, did eat their meat with gladness and singleness of heart, praising God, and having favour with all the people. And the Lord added to the church daily such as should be saved.

> **GOD WANTS TO DEMONSTRATE HOW MUCH HE LOVES IT WHEN A HOLY PEOPLE CALL OUT TO A HOLY GOD IN PURE SUBMISSION AND DEDICATION TO HIS WILL!**

What would it be like today if the Body of Christ would unify as these believers did at the beginning of the church's history, fellowshipping together, working together to reach the lost, allowing the Holy Spirit to orchestrate a move of God that Jesus would be the center of? What if pastors and leaders would pool the resources of their individual ministries and work together as one to impact their cities for the Kingdom of Christ? Things would have to change drastically for this to take place today.

The writer of Hebrews declared:

Hebrews 10:23-25
Let us hold fast the profession of our faith without wavering; (for he is faithful that promised;) and let us consider one another to provoke unto love and to good works: not forsaking the assembling of ourselves together, as the manner of some is; but exhorting one another: and so much the more, as ye see the day approaching.

God dwells within us as believers, but we are instructed not to forsake the assembling of ourselves together. We are carriers of His presence. When we, as the Body, come together, it is for the benefit of God's Kingdom. Those who are committed without wavering are those He will call to be carriers of His glory in the days ahead.

It is the Holy Spirit who convicts us, directs us, uses us, and will empower us to be the last-days army that God is raising up in the world today. Something wonderful happens when we, as a church body, come together.

> **THOSE WHO ARE COMMITTED WITHOUT WAVERING ARE THOSE GOD WILL CALL TO BE CARRIERS OF HIS GLORY IN THE DAYS AHEAD!**

CHAPTER 7

RESTORING THE TREASURES BACK TO THE CHURCH

Remember therefore from whence thou art fallen, and repent, and do the first works; or else I will come unto thee quickly, and will remove thy candlestick out of his place, except thou repent.

Revelation 2:5

I asked the Lord, "Please tell me what we can do as a last-days church to make things right. How can we see Your Kingdom come and Your will be done? What are the treasures that need to be restored back to the Church?" Here's what He answered me.

GET BACK TO THE ORIGINAL

Jesus and His disciples were our examples of how to do what God started more than two thousand years ago. Jesus' life on this earth, how He lived it and how He ministered, was our model for being effective in these last days. The disciples carried on Jesus' mission through the power of the Holy Spirit without internet, without TV or other modern technologies. The Gospel reached people and caused exponential growth in those days. Their message and the power with which it was delivered truly changed their world. The power of God was evident to those who witnessed what God was doing through them.

You may be thinking, "But we are living in a different time and a different era." Yes, I agree. What we have today gives us a tremendous advantage for the work of the Kingdom. However, technology is not supernatural. Technology must not take the place of simple humility, complete obedience to the Holy Spirit, and true compassion toward those who are lost. The disciples of Jesus didn't have the benefit of airplanes, automobiles, trains, phones, internet, or TV. They were limited in this sense, and yet they were effective. Through them, the world was being turned upside down by the Person of Jesus Christ working in and through them.

> **JESUS AND HIS DISCIPLES DIDN'T HAVE THE BENEFIT OF AIRPLANES, AUTOMOBILES, TRAINS, PHONES, INTERNET, OR TV. THEY WERE LIMITED IN THIS SENSE, AND YET THEY WERE EFFECTIVE!**

Jesus modeled simplicity and humility, yet His message was powerful and life-changing. He didn't just come with great words; He demonstrated and backed up the Word He spoke with an undeniable authority. All of Heaven was on His side. Miracles, healings, and many other signs and wonders followed His ministry. He was being directed by His heavenly Father.

John 5:19, CEV

Jesus told the people: I tell you for certain that the Son cannot do anything on his own. He can do only what he sees the Father doing, and he does exactly what he sees the Father do.

The disciples started a movement with what Jesus had modeled and the Holy Spirit directed after they were baptized in the Holy Spirit. Jerusalem was experiencing a great outpouring with three thousand coming to the Lord on the first day.

Acts 2:41

Then they that gladly received his word were baptized: and the same day there were added unto them about three thousand souls.

The apostles preached the same Word Jesus gave them to preach. There was no compromise. There was a holy fear, a reverence, causing people to be changed through repentance.

Act 2:42-44

And they continued stedfastly in the apostles' doctrine and fellowship, and in breaking of bread, and in prayers. And fear came upon every soul: and many wonders and signs were done by the apostles. And all that believed were together, and had all things common.

There was a unity that permeated the entire congregation. God was showing off through them with many signs and wonders. When persecution caused the church to spread out, the surrounding areas were then saturated with heavenly movement.

Paul, the apostle, took this Gospel to a whole new level. He was reaching both Jews and Gentiles. As he would enter a town, he would go to the Jewish synagogue and preach the message of the cross. Often, the Jewish leaders would offer great opposition, leaving Paul to find those who had an ear to hear what the Spirit was saying. He and his team would set up in the homes of those who believed in Jesus. God would show up, miracles and healings would take place, and people would come to see what was going on. What a great advertising strategy!

The early believers met on a regular basis in homes, teaching, praying for the sick and casting out demons. Then Paul would raise up leaders to take his place as overseers, because eventually the Jews would run him out of town. He duplicated himself and moved on to where the Holy Spirit told him to go next. This Gospel was so effective that the world was being transformed.

If there ever was a time for God to move, it is now. There is a stirring happening in the Body of Christ, a call for new wineskins for the new wine being poured into. Let it not be said that we backed down from our mission because we were not ready to change the way things are being done. The last seven words of a dying church are, "We never did it that way before." Now is the time to take courage and take back what the enemy has stolen from us.

There is a call to repentance that is coming straight from the throne of God. The Church is to be a glorious Church without spot or wrinkle. We should be filled to overflowing with the presence of Almighty God and the power of the Holy Spirit. Our ministries should be supernatural. Our focus should be on Jesus and how He wants us to conduct ministry.

> **IF THERE EVER WAS A TIME FOR GOD TO MOVE, IT IS NOW!**

In the midst of revival, I had a vision one morning. I saw God's thumb holding a string with a weight on it and knew it to be a plumb line. It seemed as if He was looking at something, while lining up the sting with it. The Lord then spoke to me in this vision and said, "I am now eyeballing My Church, to see if it is straight. If it is not straight, then I will tear it down to the foundation."

Then I saw a stick with markings on it. It looked old, and I knew it was the type of measuring stick used in Bible times. The Lord then spoke to me again and said, "If you measure your church with the wrong measuring stick, then you will be crooked."

When I heard this, the fear of the Lord came over me, and I asked, "What is this measuring stick, Lord?"

He said to me, "I am the measuring stick."

Jesus was telling me that if any church is not operating in His way, He will tear it down to the foundations. What a wake-up call this was to me! It changed my perception of how I should do the work of the ministry from that moment on. The Holy Spirit wants to lead us and guide us, but we must be willing to do what He wants us to do.

> "IF YOU MEASURE YOUR CHURCH
> WITH THE WRONG MEASURING STICK,
> THEN YOU WILL BE CROOKED!"

Many churches today are copying the model of so-called "successful churches," and many are going to conferences and seminars on how to successfully grow the church. We must be careful to do things the Lord's way and not just what others are doing. It is always great to learn and grow, but we need to seek the Holy Spirit for His direction for every work of God and every move of God.

Every church and body of believers is different, areas differ, and cultures differ. What works in one place may not work in others. Only the Holy Spirit knows these things.

You may be called to be unique in your ministry, different than others in the way you do what God wants you to do. He has not called us to have cookie-cutter ministries. Some ministries are designed to be small and impactful. Why, then, do we look at the church down the road and covet what that church may have? We are to be powerfully led by the Spirit to impact those whom God has called us to. God is not calling us to be successful; He is calling us to be faithful, to be faithful stewards of what He gives to us.

BECOME BALANCED BELIEVERS

Many in the Body of Christ have been turned off to the idea of supernatural manifestations in the church and what God has promised in His Word. When God begins to do what He says He will do in the church, many become negative, judgmental, and outright against what they see and hear as a move of God. The internet has opened up the communications about these things in such a way that opinions are accepted as truth, and this has caused great division in the Body of Christ.

> **GOD IS NOT CALLING US TO BE SUCCESSFUL; HE IS CALLING US TO BE FAITHFUL, TO BE FAITHFUL STEWARDS OF WHAT HE GIVES TO US!**

To say that everything that is happening in the moves of God is of God would not be honest or truthful. If we look at past moves of God, there was always a time period when there were extremes, as people got excited about what God was doing and operated without wisdom and sometimes even with silliness. Many immature seekers go overboard, focusing on one thing and trying to duplicate it in the natural. This gives the appearance that a move of God is not really of God."

At the same time, there are always those who are opposed to what is happening and who spread negative reviews, using as "proof" the extremes they have seen or heard about. We must look past the extremes of unwise individuals and see with eyes of the Spirit what God is doing in these last days.

Jesus was balanced when He did the work of the ministry. It was His compassion for the masses that caused Him to heal all who were sick. He taught the people with intensity and passion, gathering thousands at a time as people were hungry for the words of life. He trained up His disciples by teaching them, correcting them, and then allowing them to learn by doing what they had been taught. He didn't have to put on a show;

He just obeyed as His Father showed Him what to do.

The majority of Jesus' messages to the masses were in parables and were not intended to be understood unless you pursued an explanation. His words were for those who were seekers, those who were hungry to know the truth. He wasn't choosing His words carefully in fear that He might offend someone. When He said, *" Except ye eat the flesh of the Son of man, and drink his blood, ye have no life in you"* (John 6:53), some left Him saying that He was a crazy man. He asked His disciples, *"Will ye also go away?"* (verse 67).

Simon Peter answered Him, *"Lord, to whom shall we go? thou hast the words of eternal life"* (Verse 68).

Jesus was real, and He spoke with author-ity, but He also stayed humble. Often He would tell the people He healed and deliv-ered, "Don't tell anyone." He didn't seek recognition or honor. He didn't brag about what God was doing through His ministry. He didn't need to advertise, promote, or work up what would happen if the people would come to His meetings.

Jesus was very balanced in His attitude, His emotions, His speech, and His actions. He wasn't trying to prove anything to anyone. He was just doing what the Father wanted Him to do.

I think we could all learn a thing or two from Jesus. We are to be balanced believers who are led by the Spirit. We are to speak less and listen more. When we speak, we must speak with the authority God has given us. Yet, we are to stay humble in our attitudes, not thinking more highly of ourselves than we ought to think (see Romans 12:3).

Many years ago, as a young minister, I was eager to do all that God had called me to do, but sometimes I let my mouth overtake my calling. I wanted everyone to know that I was called. Looking back, I see the pride I had and the mistakes I made because of it. I am so thankful that God gave me a great wife who helped me to be balanced and showed me how to be compassionate to those who needed God's grace.

When I would attend a district meeting once a year for the denomination I was part of, it seemed to me that a lot of the pastors were in competition, trying to see who had the most people in their church. They would ask me, "So, how many people do you have in your church?" It was very disturbing to me that these men of God were so worried and curious about the numbers in other fellowships. I determined not to even answer those type of questions.

Jesus was not in competition with anyone. The numbers didn't matter to Him. He just wanted to do the will of His Father in Heaven. That is my desire too. How about you?

> **JESUS WAS NOT IN COMPETITION WITH ANYONE. THE NUMBERS DIDN'T MATTER TO HIM. HE JUST WANTED TO DO THE WILL OF HIS FATHER IN HEAVEN!**

CHAPTER 8

HOW CAN WE BE EFFECTIVE AND POWERFUL AS A CHURCH TODAY?

Let us draw near with a true heart in full assurance of faith, having our hearts sprinkled from an evil conscience, and our bodies washed with pure water. Let us hold fast the profession of our faith without wavering; (for he is faithful that promised;) and let us consider one another to provoke unto love and to good works: not forsaking the assembling of ourselves together, as the manner of some is; but exhorting one another: and so much the more, as ye see the day approaching. Hebrews 10:22-25

So, what should we do to become the last-days church that is effective and powerful before the coming of the Lord? How can we stay focused on doing what the Father wants us to do as church leaders and as believers? How can we guard our hearts from the deception that is so real today in our world and also within the four walls of our churches?

STOP PUTTING ON A SHOW!

God's People don't need to be entertained; they need to be changed, and it is only the tangible presence of Almighty God that changes us. When was the last time you took a service time to just pray? What if we didn't have electricity? Could God move without the lights, the musical instruments, and the microphones? He did it for Jesus. Keep the main thing the main thing. Focus on Jesus! We don't need to be entertained when God shows up.

GET BACK TO THE WORD THAT CUTS US TO THE CORE!

The Word challenges us to change. It stirs us to obedience and demands sacrifice. We need messages on repentance, sanctification, and holiness.

Hebrews 12:14
Follow peace with all men, and holiness, without which no man shall see the Lord.

KEEP THE MAIN THING THE MAIN THING; FOCUS ON JESUS!

We must speak truth to the lies of the culture around us. When was the last time you preached a salvation message that brought the congregation step by step to the cross? How about an altar call that required people to come forward and not be ashamed of

Jesus, an altar call in which they are crying out to God to forgive them and change them?

But won't that embarrass some people? Jesus said that if we are ashamed of Him, He will be ashamed of us before His Father:

> Mark 8:38
> *Whosoever therefore shall be ashamed of me and of my words in this adulterous and sinful generation; of him also shall the Son of man be ashamed, when he cometh in the glory of his Father with the holy angels.*

Where did we get this phrase: "We are not trying to embarrass anyone, so everyone bow your head and close your eyes?" Since when was surrendering your life to the Lord in repentance an embarrassment? The Word of God says that all of Heaven is rejoicing when one soul comes to the cross. It's time to change the way we are doing church if we expect to see a true move of God.

LET GOD MOVE IN OUR SERVICES AND STOP PUTTING A TIME LIMIT ON HIM!

If God is in the house, no one wants to go home, but when there is no true glory, the people will get restless. That is a good indicator of whether or not God is indeed "in the house." Let the Holy Spirit do what He wants to do.

In many countries, when people gather to have a church service, their services go on for most of the day and sometimes even into the night. People are so hungry for God that their ministers are expected to preach the Word for hours, not just a few minutes. In fact, there is such a hunger for the Word of God in these foreign countries that the people don't want to leave.

IF GOD IS IN THE HOUSE, NO ONE WANTS TO GO HOME, BUT WHEN THERE IS NO TRUE GLORY, THE PEOPLE WILL GET RESTLESS!

In Matthew 15, it is recorded that Jesus healed the sick and ministered to the people who came to Him, and they stayed with Him for three days straight. He feed four thousand, not including the women and children. They wanted to be with Jesus so badly that nothing was more important to them.

GET BACK TO PRAYER!

Jesus called His house *"the house of prayer"* (Mark 11:17). If we, as leaders, announce an eating meeting, everyone shows up. When we call for a prayer meeting, many stay home. Corporate prayer, these days, is little more than a past memory. Many believers don't even know how to pray because we so seldom pray together. The best way to teach a new believer how to pray is to pray together with them, giving everyone an opportunity to touch Heaven as we agree with each other in prayer.

As a body of believers, we are to war in the heavenlies together, pulling down strongholds and defeating the works of darkness. Prayer is a weapon that needs to be wielded more in these last days.

MAKE SURE OUR MINISTRIES ARE SPIRIT-FILLED AND SPIRIT-LED!

When Jesus was at the prime of His ministry, it was the Spirit's power that caused the blind to see, the lame to walk, and the dead to rise. The same Holy Spirit was poured out on the disciples so that they could be witnesses to their world. Without the Holy Spirit empowerment, they would not have been able to do all that they did for the Kingdom.

They would not have been able to demonstrate the power of God when they went to the towns and cities the Spirit led them to. It was the miracles that the Holy Spirit did through them that proved that what they were saying was actually from God Himself. We, as a church, are not effective in our world if we are not demonstrating that God is truly working through us, with signs and wonders following us.

DESIRE AND PROMOTE SPIRITUAL GIFTS!

How will the church operate in spiritual gifts if we don't teach about them. These gifts are activated in the lives of Spirit-filled believers when they have faith that these gifts are for them.

WHEN JESUS WAS AT THE PRIME OF HIS MINISTRY, IT WAS THE SPIRIT'S POWER THAT CAUSED THE BLIND TO SEE, THE LAME TO WALK, AND THE DEAD TO RISE, AND THE SAME HOLY SPIRIT WAS POURED OUT ON THE DISCIPLES SO THAT THEY COULD BE WITNESSES TO THEIR WORLD!

Romans 10:17, NKJV
Faith comes by hearing, and hearing by the word of God.

The church will not have faith to operate in the gifts if we don't teach on these gifts. Gifts are also activated by prophecy and the laying on of hands.

1 Timothy 4:14

Neglect not the gift that is in thee, which was given thee by prophecy, with the laying on of the hands of the presbytery.

As spiritual leaders, we are to teach all the Word, not just the pieces of it that suit our narrative. We are to provide every possible opportunity to make sure the church is ready and equipped for the last-days outpouring.

LET THE CHURCH BE THE TRUE BODY OF CHRIST!

The only reason that church leaders are preaching to tickle the ears of the congregation is that the church as a whole is much too fickle. People get offended by every little thing. As soon as the pastor preaches against the sins of the culture, commitment to faithfulness and holiness, or sacrificing our flesh, people are looking for another church, one that is "better suited" to their needs.

We, as believers, are not ready to die to self. Instead of becoming selfless, many are becoming ever more selfish. We leave one church because we are offended by the pastor or someone in the church and go to another congregation, bringing all our troubles with us. This is one of the reasons that the church body doesn't work together. We have burned so many bridges in the past that we are not willing go back to a church we previously attended or worked with to even visit, let alone join with the efforts of that church to reach the community for Jesus. And we wonder why the lost don't want to come to our churches?

> **IT'S TIME TO STOP PLAYING CHURCH, STOP SETTLING FOR SCRAPS, AND STOP PURSUING THINGS THAT DON'T MATTER.**

The people of the world, for the most part, have nothing to do with the church because they're not seeing authentic Christianity in us. They see us as hypocritical, judgmental, money grabbers.

In Jesus' day, the people of the world saw Him, His disciples, and the church as a whole as real, authentic, and living what they said they believed. The New Testament church was caring, full of love for one another, and signs and wonders were the normal. There was among them a unity that the world was in awe of.

We, as the Body of Christ, are so privileged to live just before the coming of the Lord. He is counting on us to come through for Him, to be the army of believers who will usher in the greatest move of God that has ever been seen on the earth.

So what must we do as individuals? It's time to stop playing church. Stop settling for scraps. Stop pursuing things that don't matter. We must be consecrated as vessels of the Lord meant to house His presence. We don't have time to play silly games. This is serious business.

Stop demanding to be entertained. The Word of God, prayer, and worship are still the foundation of our walk with the Lord. We don't need to be coddled, baby-sat or pampered. We are soldiers in the army of the living God.

In his time, Paul, the apostle, wrote a warning to those who called themselves Christians to be careful how they lived and spoke. Listen to the concerns he had for the church in those days.

Hebrews 5:11-14, TPT

*We have much to say about this topic although it is difficult to explain, because you have become too dull and sluggish to understand. For you should already be professors instructing others by now; but instead, you need to be taught from the beginning the basics of God's prophetic oracles! You're like children still needing milk and not yet ready to digest solid food. For every spiritual infant who lives on milk is not yet **pierced by the revelation of righteousness**.*

But solid food is for the mature, whose spiritual senses perceive heavenly matters. And they have been adequately *trained by what they've experienced to emerge with understanding of **the difference between what is truly excellent and what is evil and harmful.***

Two things jumped off the page at me when I read this:

1. Spiritual infants who live on milk have not yet been *"pierced by the revelation of righteousness."*

Righteousness is a product of spiritual maturity. When the church is pierced by a revelation of righteousness, men and woman alike will begin to mature in the things of God, no longer living to please themselves, but being vessels of honor for the Master's use.

2. The food for the mature is solid and they are, therefore, able to sense heavenly matters.

It takes training and experience to understand *"the difference between what is truly excellent and what is evil and harmful."* God is raising up spiritual fathers and mothers who will know how to train and equip those who are hungry and want to be used by the Lord, but will He find enough candidates? There is so little commitment on the part of modern disciples. Growing spiritually takes discipline and training. You must go through the breaking and the brokenness of heart to follow in the footsteps of Jesus. Getting prepared to be used by God is not an easy street. It will require all of you. It will require a life of surrender.

RIGHTEOUSNESS IS A PRODUCT OF SPIRITUAL MATURITY!

Many in the church today are satisfied with crumbs when we could have it all. It's all for us. Jesus paid the ultimate price for His Bride to be equipped and powerful. We are to be maturing into the Bride that He is setting apart for these last days. The church must be serious about Kingdom building. We are to be Jesus' hands and feet, and the world must know about this Jesus.

MAKE THE CROOKED PATHS STRAIGHT, AND LET REPENTANCE BE OUR DAILY BREAD!

All of the great revivals of past generations had one thing in common: repentance gripped the hearts of the seekers, and God transformed them daily. But there is very little heard from the pulpit these days about repentance. This causes many to bypass brokenness and go straight to trying to live for Jesus.

Repentance changes our direction. Without repentance people ask for forgiveness and go right back to the same sins over and over again. Repentance is a godly sorrow that is given to us by God Himself because our sin has separated us from Him.

Repentance is the fear of God that grips our hearts because we see our sin as God sees it.

As He reveals our sin to us, He lets us know how it grieves Him. When the fear of the Lord takes over, we cry out for God to change us, and He does. That is true repentance.

> **REPENTANCE CHANGES OUR DIRECTION. WITHOUT REPENTANCE PEOPLE ASK FOR FORGIVENESS AND GO RIGHT BACK TO THE SAME SINS OVER AND OVER AGAIN!**

Because there is so little repentance in the church today, we have many going to church but living like the devil when they leave. There is no power for the believer who does not repent and live a life consecrated to pleasing the Lord.

AGAIN, GET BACK TO THE WORD OF GOD!

Hebrews 12:25-27, TPT
Make very sure that you never refuse to listen to God when he speaks! For the God who spoke on earth from Sinai is the

same God who now speaks from heaven. Those who heard him speak his living Word on earth found nowhere to hide, so what chance is there for us to escape if we turn our backs on God and refuse to hear his warnings as he speaks from heaven? The earth was rocked at the sound of his voice from the mountain, but now he has promised, "Once and for all I will not only shake the systems of the world, but also the unseen powers in the heavenly realm!" Now this phrase "once and for all" clearly indicates the final removal of things that are shaking, that is, the old order, so only what is unshakeable will remain.

Hebrews states that we should not refuse to listen to the voice of the Lord when He speaks, even though it is shaking us to our core. God's Word to us today will rock our world ... if we let it. He is about to shake this world once again, and it will be His Word that does the shaking, just as He did from Mt. Sinai. But this time His Word will shake the powers of darkness, and whatever is still there after this great shaking will be the only thing remaining.

As a body of believers, we are too easily swayed by the cunning craftiness of men's words. We are too easily deceived when our belief systems are not founded on the Word of God and we don't know the Word for ourselves. We trust whatever new trend is coming along at the time and become sidetracked so easily.

No more should we allow the Word of God to be silent when men speak half truths in order to gain a crowd. No more should the Body of Christ take whatever is dished out to us by skilled craftsmen to ease our conscience into thinking that God is pleased with us when He is really not because of our compromises. It's time for those of us in the army of the living God to devour the Word of God, hear the voice of the Lord, and respond with obedience and reverence to what God is saying.

Hebrews 4:12

*For the word of God is quick, and power-ful, and **sharper than any twoedged sword**, piercing even to the dividing asunder of soul and spirit, and of the joints and marrow, and is a discerner of the thoughts and intents of the heart.*

(Emphasis Mine)

We have been given the greatest weapon the spiritual world has ever seen, and we must pick it up and use it to destroy the works of the enemy—in the church and out of the church. If the church you are attending is not preaching and teaching the whole Bible, but is leaving out parts of the Word that don't suit their narrative and doing this so as not to offend the crowd, then you need to get out of that church quickly.

If you have not been taught to repent of your sins and surrender to the lordship of Jesus Christ, then you have been lied to. It is time for us, as believers, to allow the Word of God to show us the difference between soul and spirit, so we can discern the thoughts and intents of our hearts (see Hebrews 4:12).

God's last-days army will shake this world with the Word of the living God, the Word that is uncompromised and pure, the Word that changes the hearts of men when they hear it. This living Word transforms us into what God has called us to be.

God is desiring to speak to His people once again, and when His Word transforms us and we obey that Word, we will be commissioned to preach that Word everywhere we go. It is God's Word that will shake the heavens and the earth in these last days, but it is His Church, His Bride, His army that He will use to proclaim His Word everywhere they go.

BE IN HOT PURSUIT OF GOD'S PRESENCE IN YOUR LIFE!

John 15:4-5 and 7-8, MKJV

Abide in Me, and I in you. As the branch cannot bear fruit of itself unless it remains in the vine, so neither can you unless you abide in Me. I am the Vine, you are the branches. He who abides in Me, and I in him, the same brings forth much fruit; for without Me you can do nothing.

If you abide in Me, and My Words abide in you, you shall ask what you will, and it shall be done to you. In this My Father is glorified, that you bear much fruit, so you shall be My disciples.

Our world has gotten so complicated that it is very easy for the members of the Body of Christ to get busy with their jobs, their families, and their personal pursuits and neglect what is most important. There are so many distractions in our world today. Because technology has made it possible to have easy, instant access to anything and everything we desire, it is difficult for many believers to find time to spend in prayer and in the reading and study of the Word of God.

This is why it is so important for believers today to connect to Jesus in a personal way. We need His presence in our daily lives. Everything that is given to us by God is in direct proportion to our personal connection to our heavenly Father, to Jesus, and to the Holy Spirit. This personal relationship is vital to our spiritual wellbeing, our destiny, and our ministry. How can we please God if we don't know Him, stay connected to Him, Hear His voice, and obey what He ask us to do? His presence must become very real to us and our relationship with Him must grow.

Thinking of the analogy of the vine and the branches that Jesus used (see John 15), the branch must be continuously connected to the vine in order to survive and eventually produce fruit. Many in the church today connect on Sunday and then disconnect on Monday. When Wednesday comes around, maybe they will connect again at a mid-week service. What would happen to a grape vine if the branches were cut off then grafted back on two or three days later and this was repeated every week? That branch would die and would, most certainly, never produce grapes.

This is a picture of many in the church today. They are spiritually weak, not growing, not maturing, and are therefore not being used by God. How can He use them? We cannot pick and choose when to connect to the Vine and then disconnect anytime the Christian lifestyle is not convenient for us. If we want to be mature believers, we must stay connected to the Vine, for the Vine is our Source. Jesus is our Source, and we can do nothing without Him.

> **WHAT WOULD HAPPEN TO A GRAPE VINE IF THE BRANCHES WERE CUT OFF THEN GRAFTED BACK ON TWO OR THREE DAYS LATER AND THIS WAS REPEATED EVERY WEEK?**

It is the presence of the Lord that feeds us spiritual food that produces growth in us. As a child of God, I would never want to be without His presence in my life. His presence is tangible, and we can feel the times of refreshing every time we speak His name. He has purified us with His blood, and His presence fills every empty space we create for Him.

When God speaks to us, how do we know it is God speaking? His presence confirms His words to us as truly being from Him.

Why would I not want to connect with this loving God? Am I really too busy? Can the earthly pleasures of this life compare to the glory of spending time with the God who created us?

You may be thinking, "Yeah, but I have to work."

That's not a problem. We can work while staying connected to God. He is always speaking, but are we listening? A great part of the reason why believers fall prey to this corrupt world is that they don't walk in the Spirit throughout the day.

> Galatians 5:16
> *This I say then, Walk in the Spirit, and*
> *ye shall not fulfil the lust of the flesh.*

Walking in the Spirit overrides the lust of the flesh every time. Knowing that God is with us constrains us, preventing us from wanting to sin. What if you could see Jesus in the natural, going where you are going, seeing what you are doing, at your house, on your job, at the ball field? Would you say curse words around Jesus? Would you watch the things on your phone or TV that are inappropriate for a Christian? Of course not. His presence would change the way you act, what you do, how you live.

At salvation, we invite Jesus to come into our hearts and take over. We repent of our sins, and Jesus, by His Spirit, takes up residence in us. We may not see Him, but our walk is a walk of faith. At times we feel His presence, but at other times we may not feel Him. Either way, He's there. We take Him everywhere we go. We are to live as if Christ is right there with us all the time, because He is. This is an eye-opener.

There are also tangible levels of the presence of the Lord that the believer can access as they press into God. He loves to show us that He is real. At times, when we are meditating on His Word, praying, or worshipping, God will reveal Himself to us in a tangible way. At times, His presence is so real that tears will well up in our eyes, and we can feel how much He loves us. Then there are times when His presence becomes so weighty that we are unable to even move, and He shows us His glory. Sometimes the presence of the Lord will overtake us to the point that He will allow us to share His burdens. We can feel what God feels about a situation to the point of intercession and groanings, in which only the Holy Spirit knows what we are praying.

> **WE ARE TO LIVE AS IF CHRIST IS RIGHT THERE WITH US ALL THE TIME, BECAUSE HE IS. THIS IS AN EYE-OPENER!**

Our God wants us to engage with Him fully as we worship together. He desires to speak to us, move us, touch us, equip us, and empower us. The corporate time of gathering is a great place to experience the presence of God in a greater way ... that is if we allow the Holy Spirit to have control of these services.

We must be in hot pursuit of the presence of God in our lives. It is this closeness, this connection, this relationship that God desires for His children. Don't let anything hinder you in your pursuit of God's presence.

THERE ARE TIMES WHEN GOD'S PRESENCE BECOMES SO WEIGHTY THAT WE ARE UNABLE TO EVEN MOVE, AND HE SHOWS US HIS GLORY. SOMETIMES THE PRESENCE OF THE LORD WILL OVERTAKE US TO THE POINT THAT HE WILL ALLOW US TO SHARE HIS BURDENS. WE CAN FEEL WHAT GOD FEELS ABOUT A SITUATION TO THE POINT OF INTERCESSION AND GROANINGS, IN WHICH ONLY THE HOLY SPIRIT KNOWS WHAT WE ARE PRAYING!

CHAPTER 9

FINDING HIDDEN TREASURES

My son, if thou wilt receive my words, and hide my commandments with thee; so that thou incline thine ear unto wisdom, and apply thine heart to understanding; yea, if thou criest after knowledge, and liftest up thy voice for understanding; if thou seekest her as silver, and searchest for her as for hid treasures; then shalt thou understand the fear of the LORD, and find the knowledge of God. Proverbs 2:1-5

Treasures that have been kept from the public eye will not just jump into your boat or just happen to be found without doing some serious digging. Archeologists and treasure hunters alike have proven methods of treasure hunting.

First, treasure hunters do their research. Before a hidden treasure can to be found, you need to know where to dig or where to dive. They must discover what is the most likely place they can find what they're looking for. In order to be successful, they must go back through the pages of history to uncover the secrets that no one else has found.

Next, treasure hunters must focus all of their efforts and resources on the goal of finding this hidden treasure. Being a treasure hunter will cost you something. It will cost time, money, and effort. Those who are determined will eventually find what they are looking for.

Treasure hunters must apply methods that have worked in the past in order to secure a future success. What they do, how they do it, and why they do it will effect the outcome of their pursuits.

Archeologists spend great amounts of time and resources in pursuit of treasures that have been hidden in the pages of time and hidden by the accumulation of the dirt and debris of the past. Their pursuit is an acknowledgement of just how important those hidden treasures are to preserving our past and learning from it for the future. As we look back, we can see how things used to be, for instance, how empires were started and what they did to become ancient memories that are now lost and forgotten. It is in a similar pursuit that we find the hidden truths of God's Word (the Bible).

> **BEING A TREASURE HUNTER WILL COST YOU SOMETHING. IT WILL COST TIME, MONEY, AND EFFORT. THOSE WHO ARE DETERMINED WILL EVENTUALLY FIND WHAT THEY ARE LOOKING FOR!**

The Ark of the Covenant is one of the most sought after lost treasure in the world today. Although some have claimed to have seen the Ark and know where is located, it is still hidden from all the world, tucked away in obscurity in a dark cave somewhere. I believe that the Ark of the Covenant is being preserved by God for the tribulation period. As stated in previous chapters, Jesus was God on earth, and we, as believers, are now the Ark that carries the Spirit of God wherever we go.

Past moves of God have demonstrated to us, as leaders and believers alike, that God has been at work in our recent past and is still at work today. Let us not forget these moves of God that were treasures to the Church and to the world. Let us also be in the pursuit of what God is doing today. We cannot recreate what God has done in the past, but we can learn from it and correct our current coarse because of what we have learned.

What has been among mounds of false teaching and methods of ministry must be brought back into the light so that God can move again on the Church, on our many church movements, on our nation, and in our world.

There are three hidden treasures that need to be restored to the leadership and the Body of Christ as a whole in these last days if we are to see revival in the Church and an awakening among the lost. We need these treasures. We should restore things back to the original of the book of Acts and the beginning of the Church in the days of Jesus and His early disciples. What are these hidden treasure I'm talking about? Read on.

PAST MOVES OF GOD HAVE DEMONSTRATED TO US, AS LEADERS AND BELIEVERS ALIKE, THAT GOD HAS BEEN AT WORK IN OUR RECENT PAST AND IS STILL AT WORK TODAY. LET US NOT FORGET THESE MOVES OF GOD THAT WERE TREASURES TO THE CHURCH AND TO THE WORLD!

CHAPTER 10

HIDDEN TREASURES
RESTORED: THE MESSAGE

*For the Anointed One has sent me on
a mission, not to see how many I could
baptize, but to proclaim the good news.*
1 Corinthians 1:17, TPT

The message is one of the hidden treasures
that must be restored to the leadership and
to the Body of Christ as a whole so that we
can be prepared as the last-days church God
has called us to be. That passage continues:

1 Corinthians 1:18-24, TPT
*And I declare this message stripped of
all philosophical arguments that empty*

the cross of its true power. For I trust in the all-sufficient cross of Christ alone. To preach the message of the cross seems like sheer nonsense to those who are on their way to destruction, but to us who are on our way to salvation, it is the mighty power of God released within us. For it is written:

I will dismantle the wisdom of the wise and I will invalidate the intelligence of the scholars.

So where is the wise philosopher who understands? Where is the expert scholar who comprehends? And where is the skilled debater of our time who could win a debate with God? Hasn't God demonstrated that the wisdom of this world system is utter foolishness? For in his wisdom, God designed that all the world's wisdom would be insufficient to lead people to the discovery of himself. He took great delight in baffling the wisdom of the world by using the simplicity of preaching the story of the cross in order to save those who believe it. For the Jews constantly demand to see miraculous signs, while those who are not Jews constantly cling to the world's wisdom, but we preach the crucified Messiah. The Jews stumble over him and the rest of the world sees him as foolishness. But for those who have been chosen to follow him, both Jews and Greeks, he is God's mighty power, God's true wisdom, and our Messiah.

THE MESSAGE IS ONE OF THE HIDDEN TREASURES THAT MUST BE RESTORED TO THE LEADERSHIP AND TO THE BODY OF CHRIST AS A WHOLE SO THAT WE CAN BE PREPARED AS THE LAST-DAYS CHURCH GOD HAS CALLED US TO BE!

The message that we are to preach today is powerful and yet simple. When we, as a church, proclaim what Jesus has done, what He expects of us today, and His

Kingdom principles, all of Heaven will back it up. Proclaiming and demonstrating power to deliver the demon possessed and healing the sick requires a simple but powerful message that transforms the lives of the listeners. Getting back to the Gospel will bring the Church back to its original intent.

The message of the Gospel is the power of God released within us. The Holy Spirit releases what is necessary to change hearts and lives when our message is simple yet straightforward, just as Jesus demonstrated.

Why should we ever want to change the original message of the King of Kings and the Lord of Lords? When we get back to Jesus's words and His Kingdom principles, we will begin to experience Kingdom power, power that transforms the hardest of hearts, the broken, the bruised, those who need a life change. When our message begins to line up with the original intent of the Master, we will begin to see what Jesus and His disciples saw, but in even greater measure. Why? Because the Holy Spirit and

Heaven's authority will be backing up the message we preach.

So, what is the message that has been lost to many churches and ministries today? This message is a treasure that has been obscure for such a long time, and must now be rediscovered as we are approaching the end of all things.

THE MESSAGE OF DENIAL OF SELF

Jesus said that in order for us to come after Him, we must deny ourselves. People must know that they cannot change themselves. All the self-help books and sermons will not wash away *"the sin which so easily ensnares us"* (Hebrews 12:1, NKJV). The only way to receive the great salvation that Jesus offers is to repent of our sins, recognizing that we need a Savior because we are incapable of saving ourselves.

It is through the admittance of being a sinner that we are able to call upon a Savior (Jesus). Selfishness has been the root cause of our demise as a sinner. Therefore, we must deny that selfishness and call upon a Holy God for forgiveness.

Repentance was the message of John the Baptist as he prepared the way of the Lord, and repentance is still the message needed today. Repentance prepares the way of the Lord into the hearts of each person alive, from the compromising believer to the vilest of sinners.

This message of self-denial is the catalyst for God to do His most awesome work in the hearts of those who are broken before Him. The miracle of salvation trumps all other miracles that may seem to be more spectacular to the eyes. Salvation is the miracle of our Savior who paid the full price for the sins of those who truly deny themselves through repentance and now are washed whiter than snow, all because of the blood of Jesus.

And it doesn't stop there. Salvation so transforms the life of the repentant soul that the Spirit of the living God comes to dwell deep in the heart of that believer, now known as an adopted child of God. If that doesn't excite you, I don't know what will?

Christ living in you is the hope of glory. This Christ in you defeats the power of the enemy in your life. As you continue to deny self on a daily basis, you are transformed into a vessel for the Lord's use. Your life is no longer your own; you have been bought at a great price. Now it is imperative that your self-life be crucified in order to grow, to be what God has called you to be. Your destiny is tied to this denial of self in order to please God and fulfill your calling in Him.

> **THIS MESSAGE OF SELF-DENIAL IS THE CATALYST FOR GOD TO DO HIS MOST AWESOME WORK IN THE HEARTS OF THOSE WHO ARE BROKEN BEFORE HIM!**

This message of self-denial must be preached, proclaimed, and shouted from the rooftops in order for the church to be restored back to its original state. We must see, both as leaders and believers alike, that this message is of great importance to every one of us. We must see it as the treasure it is to the last-days Church. As leaders, we must embrace this message and preach it often. As believers, we must welcome and live this message of self-denial in order to become what God has called us to be in these last days.

Denying self is not easy for those who are accustomed to following their own flesh, those who are carnal and preoccupied with this world. But in order to embrace Jesus, we must embrace this message. If there ever was a time to heed this message, it is now.

THE MESSAGE OF TAKING UP YOUR CROSS

When a believer has no ambition outside of the cross, then that believer is being led by the Spirit. It is the Spirit's leading that keeps us on track to be powerful and compassionate in a world that focuses on self. Jesus said that we must take up our cross to be able to follow Him (see Matthew 16:24).

The cross was a tool of death, a foreseen mechanism of torture that Jesus would have to endure to fulfill His purpose on the earth.

John 12:32
And I, If I be lifted up, will draw all men unto me.

The cross was the place Jesus chose to die. It was *His* cross that He carried through the streets in the sight of the masses He had preached to and possibly even healed. He willingly took up His cross.

It is the message of taking up your cross that prepares the heart of the listener to know that they must count the cost to be a follower of Jesus. This message must be restored to the last-days church to bring truth to the inward parts. This message must be preached again to establish believers on a firm foundation.

When a hungry listener knows what it takes to truly be a disciple of Jesus, then they can make a conscience decision to either accept it or reject it.

Jesus did not sugar-coat His message. His message was clear and precise.

Luke 14:26-28

If any man come to me, and hate not [love less] his father, and mother, and wife, and children, and brethren, and sisters, yea, and his own life also, he cannot be my disciple. And whosoever doth not bear his cross, and come after me, cannot be my disciple. For which of you, intending to build a tower, sitteth not down first, and counteth the cost, whether he have sufficient to finish it?

> **IT IS THE MESSAGE OF TAKING UP YOUR CROSS THAT PREPARES THE HEART OF THE LISTENER TO KNOW THAT THEY MUST COUNT THE COST TO BE A FOLLOWER OF JESUS!**

Make a life-changing decision to be willing to put Jesus as number one in your life, to love everything and everyone less than Him. To be willing even to die for Him is not a decision that should be taken lightly. That is why Jesus said we must count the cost before such a decision is made. When the leadership of our churches restore this message of the cross back to as one of the foundational truths in their preaching, everything will change. Conviction will be brought back, and God will grant repentance to those who embrace the message.

Some will resist because of the years of compromise embedded in them. Those who are not willing to hear and heed this message will have to make a decision: will they follow Jesus or not? Everyone who chooses to follow Jesus must count the cost.

If we are not willing to take up our cross, as Jesus taught, then we are not a true follower of Him.

Luke 14:27

And whosoever doth not bear his cross, and come after me, cannot be my disciple.

This message restores the church back to the original intent that Jesus and His disciples preached from the very beginning of the church age.

THE MESSAGE OF WHAT IT TAKES TO FOLLOW JESUS

Matthew 16:24
> *Then said Jesus unto his disciples, If any man will come after me, let him deny himself, and take up his cross, and follow me.*

What did it take for Jesus' disciples to follow Him? To follow Jesus they had to go where He went. Jesus didn't have a home, so He and His disciples lived as nomads. *To follow* actually means, "to be in the same path with." This message of being a follower of Jesus speaks of going where Jesus goes. We are to be led by Him and the Spirit He has given to His followers. To be a follower means that we are not going where we want to go, but going where He leads.

When we teach and preach this message of being a follower, it gives clear direction to the Body of Christ on what our focus should be (Jesus.) When He moves, we move with Him. When He stays put, we patiently wait.

Believers are not to go unless the Master goes before them. They are following Him. They must be aware of where He is and sensitive to know when He is moving.

As leaders teach this message of following Jesus, they will find that the Body of Christ will grow in maturity and do great exploits for the Kingdom. The absence of this message will cause believers to be dependent upon their leaders and on methods and strategies to lead them, causing many to be led into false teachings, powerless programs, and wrong motives.

It is this message of following Jesus that enables the Body of Christ, as individuals, to be able to be and do whatever Jesus wants of them. In the process, they become totally dependent upon Him for their direction and their stability. What a great treasure this is! And how sad that it has been missing from the mainstream of church teachings! I believe restoring this treasure back to our pulpits will transform the church in a way that will multiply the Kingdom exponentially for a last-days awakening.

To follow Jesus, the disciples had to learn from Him. They called Him *Rabbi,* which means "teacher." What Jesus taught while they were with Him was what they taught when He was not there.

This message of learning from Jesus must be restored back to the church. This will correct many years of misinterpretation of the Scriptures, bad doctrine, and outright false teaching that have too long plagued the Body of Christ.

When we get back to the teachings of Jesus, we will see a revival of truth. Jesus spoke truth to the culture of His day. Some of the first words out of His mouth were these:

Matthew 4:17
Repent for the kingdom of heaven is at hand.

Jesus taught about both Hell and Heaven, and He condemned the religious hypocrites of His day. He taught humility and love. He taught the principles of the Kingdom of God.

You and I must restore the words of Jesus back to our pulpits. There must be a revival of the simple, yet direct and confrontational teachings of Jesus.

> **THIS MESSAGE OF LEARNING FROM JESUS MUST BE RESTORED BACK TO THE CHURCH. THIS WILL CORRECT MANY YEARS OF MISINTERPRETATION OF THE SCRIPTURES, BAD DOCTRINES, AND OUTRIGHT FALSE TEACHINGS THAT HAVE TOO LONG PLAGUED THE BODY OF CHRIST!**

When the disciples were released into the world to minister, they taught what Jesus had taught them. They were eyewitnesses who had heard His words, and this had changed their lives.

To restore this message, both we as leaders and those who are following alike, must consider Jesus as our Rabbi, our Teacher, just as those early disciples did. After all, isn't Jesus the Word of God? Where, then, should we leaders get our main message of hope and redemption, if not from the words of Jesus? They are words like these:

Matthew 11:28-30

Come unto me, all ye that labour and are heavy laden, and I will give you rest. Take my yoke upon you, and learn of me; for I am meek and lowly in heart: and ye shall find rest unto your souls. For my yoke is easy, and my burden is light.

Luke 4:18-19

The Spirit of the Lord is upon me, because he hath anointed me to preach the gospel to the poor; he hath sent me to heal the brokenhearted, to preach deliverance to the captives, and recovering of sight to the blind, to set at liberty them that are bruised, to preach the acceptable year of the Lord.

Matthew 7:21

Not every one that saith unto me, Lord, Lord, shall enter into the kingdom of heaven; but he that doeth the will of my Father which is in heaven.

The Words of Jesus still ring true today. If He said it in the beginning of the Church's formation, then it must be of importance today to the last-days Church.

COME UNTO ME, ALL YE THAT
LABOUR AND ARE HEAVY LADEN,
AND I WILL GIVE YOU REST. TAKE
MY YOKE UPON YOU, AND LEARN OF
ME; FOR I AM MEEK AND LOWLY IN
HEART: AND YE SHALL FIND REST
UNTO YOUR SOULS. FOR MY YOKE IS
EASY, AND MY BURDEN IS LIGHT!

CHAPTER 11

HIDDEN TREASURES RESTORED: THE MISSION

He that committeth sin is of the devil; for the devil sinneth from the beginning. For this purpose the Son of God was manifested, that he might destroy the works of the devil.   1 John 3:8

The mission is the second hidden treasure that must be restored to the Church for the last great awakening to take place.

Motive is everything. Why do we, as the Church and as individuals, do what we do? That is a question we must be asking ourselves, as both leaders and believers.

It is easy to get off track when it comes to the mission that Jesus and His disciples had while they were here on this earth. We can get so caught up in our own agendas that we forget the real reason we do what we do for Him as a church. Our agendas can be anything from getting more numbers into our seats, raising funds that will support the ministries we want to do, or doing works of service for recognition and position. We must be careful not to disconnect from the original intent and mission of Jesus while we are trying to accomplish the goals that have been set by our ideas of what God wants us to do in ministry.

Jesus' mission was unique in a sense. He came to the earth as directed by His heavenly Father. There was a need that had to be dealt with, the need for God to restore a relationship that had been lost when Adam and Eve sinned. And God's plan was Jesus' mission.

This was why the Word of God took on the form of man and became a sacrifice for all who would believe. Jesus' life mission, as Emmanuel, was to take our place as a sin offering. To demonstrate the love that the Father had for all of humanity, Jesus took on that mission and completed what the Father had planned.

What was the mission of Jesus? Why did He come as a man? And why did He die?

Luke 19:10
For the Son of man is come to seek and to save that which was lost.

GOD'S PLAN WAS JESUS' MISSION!

It is clear from Jesus' own words that He had a mission, and that mission is unchanged today. Jesus came, lived, died, and rose again for the soul purpose of providing a way to God for those who were lost and those in pursuit of redemption and relationship with the God of creation. It was in His plan from the beginning to restore man back to his original state of intimate relationship with Father God.

When Jesus came in the flesh as a humble infant and grew up in human form and frailty, His mission was clear. He was to be the substitute, the scapegoat, the sacrifice for a lost world of people whom *"God so loved."* Everything He did was for that purpose.

Jesus then trained twelve men to continue the mission after He was gone. He stayed focused on the mission even as He was being rejected by those He came for. He demonstrated God's power with compassion for those He would redeem. Then, He laid down His life, knowing what had to be done to complete the work of salvation for those living in His time and for all those who would live in the future. This mission of Jesus was fulfilled only when He cried out on the cross. *"It is finished"* (John 19:30), and yet His mission of winning souls continues today.

Why would the Father have sent His own Son to die, why would Jesus, the Son of God, go through all that pain and rejection to fulfill the mission He had been assigned, and then change His mission after he was faithful to accomplish what the Father had given Him to do? He would not! The mission of Jesus from the beginning was to seek and to save that which was lost, and that is still the mission today. Nothing has changed. Winning the lost is still our prime directive.

The hidden treasures of this mission being restored back to the church are so vital and important to us today that we must go back to the Scriptures and compare Jesus' mission to what our mission has been as the church and individually and make necessary adjustments.

We have been chosen as Christ's ambassadors, representatives of the original mission that Jesus bled and died for. To restore the Church we must all, as leaders and believers alike, determine if what we are doing for Him is actually what He wants us to be doing. If not, let's get back on track.

What if our spiritual leaders and all believers would take on Jesus' mission as their own before the coming of the Lord? The messages in the church would change to equipping the saints to reach the lost, and the glory of God would fill us to accomplish this mission. The Holy Spirit would back up the mission with the demonstration of supernatural power.

What if everything we do as a representative of Jesus would be to reach out to the lost? This Gospel would be preached in all the world, and everyone would hear about this saving Jesus.

> **THE MISSION OF JESUS FROM THE BEGINNING WAS TO SEEK AND TO SAVE THAT WHICH WAS LOST, AND THAT IS STILL THE MISSION TODAY!**

What if our main priority would be to tell those whom we know and those God places in our path this great message of redemption through the blood of Jesus? There would be an awakening like never before. We would see our families, work associates, and friends come to a saving knowledge of Jesus Christ.

When we, as a church, and we, as believers, focus on the mission of Jesus (to seek and save that which was lost), there will be a revival in the church, and everything that we need will be provided for us so that we can reach those who are lost.

Matthew 6:33
But seek ye first the kingdom of God, and his righteousness; and all these things shall be added unto you.

When we, as the Body of Christ, focus on the mission of Christ, we will be given everything we need to accomplish His mission. God Himself will provide, and we won't have to focus on raising funds. We won't have to beg people to volunteer. When we do what God has wanted us to do from the beginning, His Church will prevail, and no devil in Hell will be able to stop it.

WHEN WE, AS THE BODY OF CHRIST, FOCUS ON THE MISSION OF CHRIST, WE WILL BE GIVEN EVERYTHING WE NEED TO ACCOMPLISH HIS MISSION. GOD HIMSELF WILL PROVIDE, AND WE WON'T HAVE TO FOCUS ON RAISING FUNDS. WE WON'T HAVE TO BEG PEOPLE TO VOLUNTEER. WHEN WE DO WHAT GOD HAS WANTED US TO DO FROM THE BEGINNING, HIS CHURCH WILL PREVAIL, AND NO DEVIL IN HELL WILL BE ABLE TO STOP IT!

CHAPTER 12

HIDDEN TREASURES RESTORED: THE MANIFESTATIONS

And these signs shall follow them that believe. Matthew 16:17

The manifestations of the Holy Spirit is the last hidden treasure that must be restored to the Body of Christ, His Church, to bring about a great awakening of the masses that has been foretold in the Scriptures. That full passage says:

Mark 16:15-20
And he [Jesus] said unto them, Go ye into all the world, and preach the gospel

to every creature. He that believeth and is baptized shall be saved; but he that believeth not shall be damned. And these signs shall follow them that believe; In my name shall they cast out devils; they shall speak with new tongues; they shall take up serpents; and if they drink any deadly thing, it shall not hurt them; they shall lay hands on the sick, and they shall recover.

So then after the Lord had spoken unto them, he was received up into heaven, and sat on the right hand of God. And they went forth, and preached everywhere, the Lord working with them, and confirming the word with signs following.

Yes, the last treasure to be restored is the manifestations that God demonstrates as His Church does what He wants us to do. These manifestations happen automatically as a direct result of preaching the message Jesus instructed His disciples to preach and being focused on the mission that Jesus gave them to accomplish.

Jesus wants His Church to be powerful yet purposeful. He has given to every believer a mandate. That mandate is called the Great Commission.

GO INTO ALL THE WORLD AND PREACH THE GOSPEL TO EVERY CREATURE!

We are not in charge of the results; God is. We are just to obey Him.

We are called to obey this mandate still today. Nothing has changed from when Jesus gave these instructions to His followers on the day He was to leave this earth in a cloud of glory.

> **THESE MANIFESTATIONS HAPPEN AUTOMATICALLY AS A DIRECT RESULT OF PREACHING THE MESSAGE JESUS INSTRUCTED HIS DISCIPLES TO PREACH AND BEING FOCUSED ON THE MISSION THAT JESUS GAVE THEM TO ACCOMPLISH!**

When we are obedient to do what Jesus wants us to do, He will demonstrate through us manifestations of power to those we preach to, with signs and wonders following our obedience. It is our obedience that brings the authority and proof in the form of supernatural manifestations. We will, as believers, experience a supernatural move of God on our behalf when we preach what Jesus told us to preach to the ones He told us to preach to.

Every believer can do greater works than Jesus did on the earth because He gave us His Spirit as a baptism of His power and authority.

John 14:12-14

Verily, verily, I say unto you, He that believeth on me, the works that I do shall he do also; and greater works than these shall he do; because I go unto my Father. And whatsoever ye shall ask in my name, that will I do, that the Father may be glorified in the Son. If ye shall ask any thing in my name, I will do it.

These are the times in which God wants to pour out His Spirit on *"all flesh"* (Joel 2:28). He wants a Church without spot or wrinkle. He is also wanting a Church filled with the power and authority to restore the treasures of the Kingdom to a world in need of a Savior.

> **WHEN WE ARE OBEDIENT TO DO WHAT JESUS WANTS US TO DO, HE WILL DEMONSTRATE THROUGH US MANIFESTATIONS OF POWER TO THOSE WE PREACH TO, WITH SIGNS AND WONDERS FOLLOWING OUR OBEDIENCE!**

Paul wrote:

1 Corinthians 2:1-5
And I, brethren, when I came to you, came not with excellency of speech or of wisdom, declaring unto you the testimony of God. For I determined not to know anything among you, save Jesus Christ, and him crucified. And I was with you in weakness, and in fear, and

in much trembling. And my speech and my preaching was not with enticing words of man's wisdom, but in demonstration of the Spirit and of power: that your faith should not stand in the wisdom of men, but in the power of God.

Authority is given to those who are baptized in the Spirit and are obedient to fulfill the mission that Jesus set forth before He left us His Holy Spirit.

The disciples were with Jesus for three and a half years. They saw the miracles, they heard Jesus' teaching, and they were given authority to go out as His apostles. He gave them their last instructions just before He left them:

Acts 1:4-5

And, being assembled together with them, commanded them that they should not depart from Jerusalem, but wait for the promise of the Father, which, saith he, ye have heard of me. For John truly baptized with water; but ye shall be baptized with the Holy Ghost not many days hence.

Act 1:8

But ye shall receive power, after that the Holy Ghost is come upon you: and ye shall be witnesses unto me both in Jerusalem, and in all Judaea, and in Samaria, and unto the uttermost part of the earth.

The disciples were instructed by Jesus to wait for the promised Holy Spirit baptism. Ten days after Jesus left them, they were in an upper room waiting and praying, and the Holy Spirit was poured out upon them in a great way.

If this was important for Jesus' disciples then, it is still important for us to be endued with power from on high in order to be a witness in our world today. This empowerment of the Holy Spirit is the catalyst for the manifestations of the Spirit to be activated in each believer, so we can be an effective witness in our world.

When we combine the right message with the right mission, it is the Spirit of God that will produce the manifestations of the supernatural signs and wonders to prove that what is being said is from God Himself.

IF THIS WAS IMPORTANT FOR JESUS' DISCIPLES THEN, IT IS STILL IMPORTANT FOR US TO BE ENDUED WITH POWER FROM ON HIGH IN ORDER TO BE A WITNESS IN OUR WORLD TODAY!

It is the simple yet powerful message that transforms the life of an unbeliever, as the Holy Spirit reveals that God is at work. This is what will bring about such a demonstration of God's power that it will change the coldest and darkest heart. It is the manifestations of the Spirit that reveal the love of God in action.

When people are set free from demons, when the blind are able to see, when short legs grow out, and arms supernaturally appear as unbelievers watch, it changes their hearts. When the world sees how great God's love is for them, people take notice. When the dead are raised to life and cancer is completely healed, unbelievers quickly become believers. It is the combination of truth and compassion that will grip the hearts of the broken.

If there ever was a time to pursue this, it is now. Our world is ripe for a great awakening. As the world gets darker and darker, it is the light of God's glorious Gospel that will shine forth with all the power and authority of Heaven to finally see God's Kingdom come and His will be done on Earth as it is in Heaven.

One morning very recently, when I was in church, the glory of the Lord was so evident and present. During the worship time, a portal was opened above me, and I could see into Heaven and what was going on there. I saw an enormous host of angels all standing facing Jesus, who was in the center. There was excitement in the air. I could see and feel that all of Heaven was with great anticipation. The angels were excited, and

Jesus was pointing to individual angels, giving them assignments. As they received their assignments, they would immediately fly off to do what Jesus had told them to do. The others were all eagerly waiting to hear what Jesus wanted them to do.

Then, suddenly, all activity stopped. Jesus turned and looked at me and said with a load roar, "It's harvest time!"

Right now, all of Heaven is standing at attention. The great cloud of witnesses is anticipating what God will do next in the earth. There is an excitement in the heavenlies that Jesus is coming soon. We don't have much time to waste. It's harvest time!

"IT'S HARVEST TIME!"

Restoring the treasures back to the Church will bring about such a change that our churches will be filled to overflowing. Our ministries will have to change because of the numbers of new believers that will inundate our systems of normal church activity. What happens when the church has added three thousand souls in one day? Are we ready for such an onslaught of hungry people? Will what we are doing now be good enough to raise up the needed army of new believers?

Luke 5:36-39, TPT

And he gave them this illustration: "No one rips up a new garment to make patches for an old, worn-out one. If you tear up the new to make a patch for the old, it will not match the old garment. And who pours new wine into an old wineskin? If someone did, the old wineskin would burst and the new wine would be lost. New wine must always be poured into new wineskins. Yet you say, 'The old ways are better,' and you refuse to even taste the new that I bring."

There is a new move of God coming, and the way we are doing things right now must change so that we will be able to receive this new wave of revival and awakening. The wineskin of our methods and systems of doing church must change if we are to be ready for what God is about to do in the near future.

These timeless treasures must be restored back to the church to prepare the way and get ready for what is coming. Every believer is needed in the coming move of God. We, as leaders, must get the church ready. We, as believers, must commit to being ambassadors at the end of this age. We are God's Church, His Bride, and there is nothing He will not do to prepare us for His soon return.

> **WE ARE GOD'S CHURCH, HIS BRIDE, AND THERE IS NOTHING HE WILL NOT DO TO PREPARE US FOR HIS SOON RETURN!**

AUTHOR CONTACT INFORMATION

Billy Webre
214 Julies Street
Gray, LA 70359-4922

Phone 985-991-0079
Email: bwebre42@yahoo.com

Facebook pages:
Billy Webre or
Back from the Brink (group)

www.ingramcontent.com/pod-product-compliance
Lightning Source LLC
LaVergne TN
LVHW011327080426
835513LV00006B/234